S0-DGK-669

# Change and Resilience in Fishing

# Change and Resilience in Fishing

**Edited by Susan Hanna and Madeleine Hall-Arber**

Oregon Sea Grant  Corvallis, Oregon

ORESU-B-00-001

© 2000 by Oregon State University. All rights reserved.

ISBN 1-881826-23-6

Oregon Sea Grant
Oregon State University
402 Kerr Administration Bldg.
(541) 737-2716

## Support

This publication was funded by the NOAA Office of Sea Grant and Extramural Programs, U.S. Department of Commerce, under grant number NA36RG0451 (project number M/A-13), and by appropriations made by the Oregon State legislature.

Sea Grant is a unique partnership with public and private sectors, combining research, education, and technology transfer for public service. This national network of universities meets the changing environmental and economic needs of people in our coastal, ocean, and Great Lakes regions.

## Credits

*Editor:* Sandy Ridlington
*Cover:* Monica Whipple

# Contents

# Acknowledgments

The work of individual contributors to this book was funded as follows:

Rollie Barnaby—Maine-New Hampshire Sea Grant, grant number NA56RG0159, project number A/P-1

Joseph Cone—Oregon Sea Grant, grant number NA36RG0451, project number M/A-12

Flaxen D. L. Conway—Oregon Sea Grant, grant number NA36RG0451, project number A/FDF-1

Lori A. Cramer—Oregon Sea Grant, grant number NA36RG0451, project number R/FDF-3

Jennifer Gilden and Jan Auyong—Oregon Sea Grant, grant number NA36RG0451, project number M/A-1

Madeleine Hall-Arber—MIT Sea Grant, grant number NA46RG0434, project number A-3

Susan Hanna—Oregon Sea Grant, grant number NA36RG0451, project number R/FDF-6

Laurie Houston, Rebecca Johnson, Ed Waters, Hans Radtke, and John Gates—Oregon Sea Grant, grant number NA36RG0451, project number R/FDF-4

Helen J. Mederer and Christopher Barker—Rhode Island Sea Grant, grant number NA36RG0503, project number R/SS-931

R. Bruce Rettig—Oregon Sea Grant, grant number NA36RG0451, project number R/FDF-1

Courtland L. Smith, Joseph Cone, Jennifer Gilden, Brent S. Steel—Oregon Sea Grant, grant number NA36RG0451, project number R/FDF-2

Anisa M. Zvonkovic, Lori A. McGraw, and Margaret Manoogian-O'Dell—Oregon Sea Grant, grant number NA36RG0451, project number R/FDF-5

# CHAPTER 1

# Introduction

*Susan Hanna and Madeleine Hall-Arber*

Marine fisheries exist in an environment of change. Cycles of growth and decline occur naturally in fish populations, seafood markets, and general economic activity onshore. Regulations controlling the use of fishery resources vary as biological and economic conditions change.

People, communities, and regions depend on fisheries for economic and social benefits. Fisheries generate these benefits through processing and sale, through recreation and tourism, and through the cultural and aesthetic environment of coastal regions. The degree of dependence on the benefits that fisheries provide determines how acutely coastal businesses, communities, and regions experience the impact of cycles of expansion and decline.

The Pacific Northwest and New England have long traditions in fishing. The economic and social heritage of both regions has been enriched by fishing history, and the two regions have lived through many periods of fishery change.[1] In this and in fishing industry characteristics they have much in common. The fishing industries in the Pacific Northwest and New England are heterogeneous in target species, gear, vessels, scale of processing, and marketing. Both industries are peopled with members who are diverse in income, education, and culture, and both are struggling to develop operational definitions of sustainable use.[2]

There are also important differences between the Pacific Northwest and New England regions. The detailed geography of the New England

1

coastline, with its many ports and islands, contrasts with the relatively flat Pacific Northwest coast, whose few ports face open ocean. The historical patterns of ethnic settlement differ, with New England retaining areas of strong ethnic association that the Pacific Northwest has left behind. The 400-year history of New England fisheries contrasts with the 150-year Pacific history. Fishery management styles in the two regions also vary, with a greater attention to a business style in the Pacific and a more cultural style in New England.

Recent years have brought dramatic change to the fisheries of the Pacific Northwest and New England. After the rapid expansions of the late 1970s and early 1980s, fisheries in both regions are now experiencing scarcity and decline. Some fisheries are in crisis; many Northwest salmon stocks are threatened or endangered, and certain of the New England groundfish stocks are at historically low levels. Other fisheries, such as Pacific groundfish, are under severe economic pressure as overcapitalized fleets cope with requirements to rebuild overfished stocks. Fisheries in both regions are experiencing sharp reductions in allowable catch, increasingly complicated regulations, and severe curtailments of fishing effort. Conflict and confusion abound.

Fishing businesses, families, communities and managers are all experiencing the economic and social impacts of fishery decline. Fishery access is increasingly limited and regulations are more restrictive. Earnings from fishing are in decline, jobs are lost, and coastal economies suffer. In coastal counties, where fishing can generate up to 25 percent of total earned income, these economic impacts are significant.[3] The accompanying social impacts, although sometimes less visible, are correspondingly large.

One of the intriguing aspects of fisheries is that they are never static. While fishery declines continue to have a severe impact on some communities and fisheries, others are showing signs of recovery. In fisheries such as New England scallops and haddock, the fish stocks are rebounding; in others, such as Pacific groundfish, stocks will be slower to recover because of their different life histories. In a few New England fisheries, high fish prices and low fuel costs have allowed some fishing families and communities to maintain a semblance of their way of life, despite restrictions that would otherwise force its abandonment.

The 1996 Sustainable Fisheries Act introduced significant changes to the conduct of fishery management. It strengthens prohibitions against overfishing and requires the rebuilding of overfished stocks, reduction of bycatch, protection of essential fish habitat, and assessment of impacts on fishing communities. These changes are the culmination of 23 years of federal fishery management experience under the regional fishery management councils. They reflect changing public attitudes toward fisheries.

The Sustainable Fisheries Act emphasizes the biological goals of management and the need to protect and recover fish stocks. But it also acknowledges that fisheries include important human resources. How will people respond to these changes? How will fishers, fishing families, fishing communities and regions be affected by fishery declines and recoveries? How resilient will they be?

Information on the human components of fisheries is critical to fishery managers faced with hard decisions, but it is rarely available. Who are the people who catch and process fish and work in coastal businesses? What is the nature of the changing environment in which they live and work? How are families, businesses, and ports responding to resource decline? What is the role of public policy in addressing that decline? What is the economic history of fishing regions, and what are the economic impacts of various policy options? How are the people who are experiencing the decline being helped and by what private and public institutions? What are the assistance successes and unmet needs?

This collection of papers begins to answer these questions by looking at fishing families, communities, and regions in their resource contexts and by examining some of the difficult challenges of management and integrated research, outreach, and communication necessary to support it. The authors address social and economic questions at different scales: regions, state and federal government, communities, fishing businesses, and families. They describe postwar change in New England and the Pacific, identify the costs and benefits of change, look at how values affect responses to change, assess the role of skills development in coping with change, and describe the challenges of interdisciplinary research coordination and communication. The writers offer the different perspectives of anthropology, resource economics, family studies, sociology, outreach, administration, and communications. Together they represent extensive collective experience with the human components of fisheries and other natural resource systems.

The papers are organized by scale of activity—regions, communities, and families—and by management concern—loss and compensation, and the integration of research, outreach, and communication.

# Changes: Regional, Community, and Family Perspectives

## Regions

Hanna takes a historical look at the groundfish fisheries of New England and the Pacific, focusing on the postwar period as a time of rapid change. She looks in particular at the institutional change introduced by the 1976 Fishery Conservation and Management Act, and the way the two regions responded differently to this change. The resilience of management has differed in the two regions, in part because of conditions at the point of management implementation, the location of threats, and styles of management.

Houston et al. examine the economic contribution of fishing in New England and the Pacific Northwest. They present similarities and differences in the two fishing regions, looking at the economic impacts of declines in fish populations and catch and comparing the impacts on households and governments. Their paper points to the need for policymakers to account for the various components of regional economies. Assessments of this type illustrate the distribution of impacts, which will help address questions of equity.

## Communities

Hall-Arber looks at the different responses to change in two Massachusetts fishing ports, examining why one port functions more effectively as a fishing community than the other. She identifies the importance of a sense of identity, educational processes, and opportunities to air different points of view and develop consensus. She concludes that communities are not homogeneous entities, that they are not always well represented in fishery management, and that fishery managers need much more knowledge about them.

Cramer discusses how rural residents often lack the human and social capital to adapt to social change. Looking at fishing-dependent communities in Oregon, she examines the importance of commercial fishing among residents and its implication for human capital development options. The people she interviewed felt that commercial fishing would be less important in the future than it was in the past. Development of human capital in marketable skills and a move toward economic diversity are necessary adaptations to the changing role of fisheries that will require structural support as well as individual aspirations.

## Families

Mederer and Barker point to the importance of understanding the social consequences of fishery management by looking at the impacts of fishery regulation on families in Point Judith, Rhode Island. They identify management actions that have eroded the Point Judith fishing community and identify several factors that work against its re-creation: a lack of planning for future fishing industry workers, misunderstanding between fishers and managers, and a lack of reward for innovation.

Zvonkovic et al. focus on family relationships in fishing communities, concluding that it is important for fishery managers to recognize the diversity in fishing families and to include the wives in commercial fishing families in their consideration of the industry. They argue that retraining programs for the fishing industry should account for the unique nature of fishing and the adaptations of fishing families. Building links between fishery management, families, and communities would have important benefits.

Conway recognizes the challenge fisheries management presents through its requirements for information and its frequent adjustments. Fishing families are independent, prizing autonomy and quick decision making, both at sea and onshore. Resilience, innovation, and endurance have been key coping mechanisms for the fishing industry, but traditional coping mechanisms may no longer be effective. She describes the fishing families outreach project designed to empower fishing businesses and families to manage change and transition and to become more effective participants in fishery management.

## Management Challenges

### Loss and Compensation

Smith et al. examine the impact of the 1994 coastwide closure of recreational fisheries for coho salmon. The closure resulted from years of complex interactions among many factors that continue to create problems for those still fishing. They see growing public concern about the future of salmon, pointing to changes in regional priorities, government actions, agency rhetoric, and fishers' behaviors. Community action to restore watershed habitat will be a test of how important salmon are to the Pacific Northwest culture.

Rettig examines two debates engendered by the salmon crisis: Can we end decline of salmon stocks and, if so, how? Who should bear the cost of salmon decline and recovery? He looks at the Conservation Reserve Enhancement Program to understand what has happened and why enhancement is controversial. He identifies compensation as a valuable tool in fishery management and the restoration of salmon habitat that can reduce conflict and let managers focus on technical problems of biology and physical processes.

### Integrating Research, Outreach, and Communication

Barnaby addresses one of the problems of fishery management in New England: the tendency of various parties to work alone, without connection to others. The fishing industry, feeling excluded from management, has an interest in more participatory forms of management but may not realize the amount of work involved. He describes various ongoing approaches to participatory management in New England, noting the benefits of participation in incorporating local knowledge and reflecting industry diversity.

Cone reexamines the idea of the passive audience as he looks at communication as a tool to create change. Empowerment involves giving people access to the powerful tools of communication. He describes three recent communication efforts that have involved the audience as producers: fishing family newsletters, letters to fishing families, and a fishing family video. All three projects were experiments in co-production, with lessons for all about context and priorities in the communication of ideas.

Gilden and Auyong describe the Adapting to Change research and outreach project sponsored by Oregon Sea Grant in light of the challenges it posed to creating an interdisciplinary project. The project achieved a cross-disciplinary perspective but not interdisciplinary integration. They present lessons learned about interdisciplinary programs, identifying the need for a common culture among researchers and outreach practitioners, a tradition of close communication and proximity, and strong commitment to production of a seamless product.

## Conclusion

Changes in the ecological, economic, and regulatory status of fisheries affect those associated with or dependent on them. Change is inevitable in fisheries, their organization, and management, and consideration of the social and economic aspects of change will lead to more effective and equitable management systems. This volume takes a multidisciplinary look at the human dimensions of fishery changes. The focus is on consequence and response, but our goal is to suggest directions for future research and outreach that will lead to improvements in management and resilience in fisheries in times of both decline and recovery.

# Notes

1. D. J. White, 1954, *The New England Fishing Industry: A Study in Price and Wage Settin*g (London: Oxford University Press); C. L. Smith, 1979, *Salmon Fishers of the Columbia* (Corvallis, OR: Oregon State University Press); M. E. Dewar, 1983, I*ndustry in Trouble: The Federal Government and the New England Fisheries* (Philadelphia: Temple University Press); A. F. McEvoy, 1986, *The Fisherman's Problem: Ecology and Law in the California Fisheries* (Cambridge: Cambridge University Press); I. Martin, 1994, *Legacy and testament: The story of the Columbia River Gillnetters* (Pullman, WA: Washington State University Press); R. A. Carey, 1999, *Against the Tide: The Fate of the New England Fisherman* (Boston: Houghton Mifflin Company).

2. M. Hall-Arber, 1993, *Social Impact Assessment of Amendment #5 to the Northeast Multispecies Fishery Management Plan: Interim Report.* MIT Sea Grant report 93-25 (Cambridge, MA: MIT Sea Grant); and Jennifer Gilden, ed., 1999, *Oregon's Changing Coastal Fishing Communities* (Corvallis, OR: Oregon Sea Grant).

3. H. D. Radtke and S. W. Davis, 1993, *Economic Description of Coastal Fisheries in the Pacific Northwest* (Newport, OR: Oregon Coastal Zone Management association).

# Part 1

## Changes: Regional, Community, and Family Perspectives

# Regions

# CHAPTER 2

# Change and Resilience in New England and Pacific Groundfish Fisheries

*Susan Hanna*

## Introduction

Twenty-three years after the implementation of the Fishery Conservation and Management Act (FCMA), U.S. fishery management is under unprecedented scrutiny. Change is widespread. Overcapacity of fishing fleets has decreased economic productivity and increased management conflict. The public owners of the fishery resources are growing less tolerant of resource overuse and are insisting that healthy, diverse marine ecosystems be maintained. New legal provisions have required a more precautionary approach to management. In the Pacific, ocean productivity has been changed by El Niño and La Niña and other oceanographic events that alter food availability to fish populations.

Fishery managers and the fishing industry are trying to cope with these changes. Managers are challenged to devise regulations that will end overfishing, rebuild fish stocks, reduce bycatch, account for essential fish habitat, and assess impacts on fishing communities. The fishing industry is attempting to find ways to reduce fishing capacity, restore fishery profitability, and keep the impacts of fishing within acceptable bounds.

The New England and Pacific fishing regions share these challenges. Change and adaptation are on many minds. This paper is about how the two regions—through their management structures, management procedures, and styles of user-group participation—have responded differently to change. Some responses have built management resilience; others have diminished it. New England and the Pacific are studies in contrast in their responses to change, the resilience of their management, and the paths they have taken.

## Change, Adaptation, and Resilience in Fisheries

Processes of change, adaptation, and resilience underlie all fisheries. Change is continual and multifaceted, including ecological variability, market dynamics, technological innovations, and shifts in public attitudes. Change also includes the evolution of institutions—the rights, rules, and responsibilities under which fishery management decisions are made.

Fishery participants often distinguish change in terms of its frequency. Some types of change are considered normal because they are frequent or at least predictable, whereas others are considered anomalous because they are more gradual or sporadic. Ecological, technological, and market changes are considered by most fishery participants to be normal types of change because they have historically characterized fishery operations. Participants have adapted to their existence. In contrast, changes in public attitudes and institutions may be seen as anomalous because they happen less frequently and represent shifts in the basic conditions under which fisheries operate.

Change in fisheries is both expansionary and contractionary. The 1976 passage of the FCMA has been perhaps the largest change affecting U.S. fishery management in the postwar period. It extended U.S. fishing territory to 200 miles offshore and established an entirely new participatory form of fishery management. It opened an era of expansionary change for U.S. fisheries, actively promoted by the government. More recently, also with government support, change has been more contractionary, requiring downward adjustments in expectations and use.

Adaptation is an adjustment to changing circumstances, one of the tasks required of all organisms and organizations if they are to survive. Resilience is the ability to maintain essential functions in the face of change. It is a concept that applies to both natural and human systems. Resilience in fishery management means the ability to maintain the functions of conservation and allocation when external changes occur. These functions include activities such as information gathering and analysis, coordination of decisions, program design, implementation of regulations, and enforcement.

Resilience depends on successful adaptation to change. Regional fishery management adaptations have varied in their success during the post-World War II period and have led to different degrees of management resilience. Each incremental adaptation establishes baseline conditions over which the next change is layered, creating, over time, a path of development.

## Current Status of New England and Pacific Groundfish Fisheries

In its *Report to Congress: Status of Fisheries of the United States*, the National Marine Fisheries Service summarizes what is known about the status of U.S. fish stocks.[1]

The New England Fishery Management Council includes 21 groundfish species in its Northeast Multispecies Fishery Management Plan. Of these, 8 are overfished, 2 are approaching an overfished condition, 6 are neither overfished nor approaching an overfished condition, and 5 are unknown. A moratorium on new entry into the groundfish fleet has been in place since 1994, and federally funded vessel buyback programs have been operational since 1995.[2] The adoption of Amendment 5 to the Multispecies Plan in 1994 followed by Amendment 7 in 1997 introduced the strictest regulatory controls in New England management history. The goal was to limit overfishing and rebuild the spawning potential of the stocks.[3] Crises in the major groundfish stocks (cod, haddock, and yellowtail flounder) have forced such stringent management responses.[4]

It is a time of contraction in Pacific groundfish fisheries as well, although at less severe levels than in New England. The Pacific Fishery Management Council includes 82 species in the Groundfish Fishery Management Plan. Of these, none are overfished, 5 are approaching an overfished condition, 10 are neither overfished nor approaching an overfished condition, 1 is not overfished (but we don't know whether it is approaching an overfished condition), and 67 are unknown. Recently, large reductions in catch have been required to prevent overfishing. For example, total allowable catches of rockfish (*Sebastes* spp.) were reduced by between 22 and 77 percent between 1996 and 1997, followed by further cuts in 1998.[5]

In both regions, overcapacity is a fundamental problem. There are too many vessels chasing too few fish. The combination of declining fish stocks and high levels of fishing capacity has meant there are fewer fish available to fishing capital and labor. In New England, two federally funded vessel buyback programs have been conducted: a $2 million pilot program, followed by a $25 million expanded program.[6] In the Pacific, the trawl sector has initiated an industry-funded vessel buyback program, now under Department of Commerce review.

## New England and Pacific Fishery Management in the Postwar Period

A look back over the postwar period to how the fisheries in the two regions developed reveals that large differences in groundfish fishery status between New England and the Pacific can be traced at least in part to how the two regions adapted to change. Changes affecting the New England and Pacific groundfish fisheries fall roughly into three periods: postwar expansion (late 1940s to 1950s), protection and enclosure (1960s to 1970s), and contraction and decline (1980s to 1990s).

### Postwar Expansion—1940–1950s

Immediately after World War II the New England and the Pacific fisheries were poised for expansion. Strong wartime markets, vessels reconverted from war use to fishing, and new technology combined with postwar optimism to drive expectations of government and industry alike toward expansion. Fishing capacity increased on both coasts. Fisheries were developed in new areas and landings increased, only to be followed soon thereafter by falling prices and, in some cases, concerns about overfishing.[7] Overall, stocks were in fairly good condition, although there were concerns about bycatch of juvenile fish. Assessments of stock condition were limited in both number and methodology.[8] In this period, New England and the Pacific shared similar fishery change and response.

### Protection and Enclosure—1960–70s

In the 1960s and 1970s the paths of New England and the Pacific began to diverge. The geographic expansion of fisheries continued, with new fisheries being developed by increasingly mobile and powerful fleets. The waters off New England were subjected to extremely high levels of fishing by distant-water fleets of 15 countries during the 1960s and early 1970s.[9] This increased activity caused severe stock depletions and international conflicts over quota allocations among members of the International Commission for the Northwest Atlantic Fisheries. Foreign fishing was active off the Pacific coast as well, although not as intense as that in the northwest Atlantic.[10]

By the 1960s concern about the competitive position of U.S. fleets was widespread. U.S. vessels were outdated and could not compete with the foreign vessels offshore. Seafood imports were at all-time highs, having increased from 37 to 76 percent of total seafood supply between 1958 and 1968.[11] Controls over foreign fleets were considered inadequate to protect U.S. interests.[12] Senator Warren Magnuson, speaking to a 1968 conference on the future of the U.S. fishing industry, characterized U.S. fisheries as having "fallen into a decade of drift."[13]

Interest in removing foreign fishing from northeast and northwest waters led eventually to the passage of the FCMA. In 1976 the FCMA expanded the exclusive fishing zone to 200 miles and established a new institutional arrangement for fisheries in eight regional fishery management councils. Through the councils the management of fisheries in state and federal waters was formally coordinated for the first time. The FCMA significantly changed the rules, the participants, and the structure within which U.S. fisheries were to be managed.

The response of the fisheries to the FCMA and its regional council structure was expansion. The "get the foreigners out" sentiment driving the passage of the FCMA continued in the form of high expectations for fisheries growth in both the New England and Pacific regions. Government incentive programs fueled the growth. In both regions fishing capacity increased rapidly in the face of these expectations and incentives. But the response of fisheries management was, in contrast, quite different in the two regions. The new council system was layered onto existing state and interstate management structures, and it is in this structure that regional differences most strikingly emerged.

The five states of the New England region were diverse and represented many interests.[14] They shared a skepticism about federal control and a desire to maintain the tradition of individualism and freedom in fisheries. But they differed in goals for the fishery and failed to craft a common identity. As a consequence, the New England Fishery Management Council created only a minimal organizational structure and took a hands-off approach to managing fisheries. A high value was placed on maximizing the flexibility of individual fishing operations.

In contrast, the Pacific region entered the new system with a history of interstate coordination and decision making, broad general acceptance of government's role in the regulation of public resources, and a history of industry and government cooperation in research. The Pacific region adapted easily to the corporate organizational structure of the new council system, setting up a full range of advisory committees and building on existing interstate coordination. Providing flexibility to fishers was also important in the Pacific region, but the abundance of lightly fished resources provided an important cushion for this flexibility that the New England region did not have.

## Contraction and Decline: 1980–90s

By the 1980s and 1990s the momentum of the post-FCMA expansion had led to a period of diminished and frustrated expectations. These decades have been characterized by increased fishing pressures, overcapacity, conflicts over rights and the allocation of catch, declining regulatory legitimacy, increasing visibility of environmental interests, and questions about the integrity of the science used as a basis for decision making.

Despite clear evidence in the 1960s that New England's fisheries had been overexploited by foreign fleets, the domestic fishery continued its post-FCMA expansion until 1985. Frustrated with the poor enforcement of quotas, the New England Fishery Management Council abandoned their use in 1982 in favor of input controls such as minimum fish size, mesh size, and closed areas. Free entry without output controls resulted in continued overexploitation of fish stocks. In 1991 the Conservation Law Foundation and the Massachusetts Audubon Society sued the U.S. Department of Commerce for allowing overfishing of cod, haddock, and yellowtail flounder, the three most important commercial groundfish species.[15] By 1990, these species had declined sharply in the Gulf of Maine, ending fisheries that had been conducted for hundreds of years.[16] Even so, resistance to placing limits on entry into the fishery continued until 1994, when a moratorium on vessel permits was included in Amendment 5 to the FMP.[17]

The Pacific groundfish fishery also continued to expand until the 1980s. The fishery was regulated by a combination of input controls (mesh size, seasons, minimum fish size) and output controls (harvest guidelines and trip limits). The industry initiated a license limitation program in 1986 that was finally implemented it in 1992.[18] Industry participation in the council process had been regular and systematic since early council implementation, so knowledge of and support for regulatory controls were strong.[19] Nevertheless, conflict increased as previously "virgin" stocks were fished down to levels that required reductions in landings. This period saw an increase in the participation and influence of environmental organizations on advisory panels and at council meetings.

For the U.S. as a whole, the 1990s saw the realization of one of the original FCMA goals: the continued reduction of seafood imports as a percentage of total supply. In 1991, another goal was achieved when foreign fishing and processing were completely eliminated from the exclusive economic zone.[20] But concern about how to address the social and cultural impacts of fishery restrictions was growing, as was public unease with the overexploitation of fisheries. These concerns created political momentum that led in 1996 to the passage of the Sustainable Fisheries Act (SFA), which amended the Magnuson Fishery Conservation and Management Act (MFCMA) by introducing more stringent environmental controls. Much tighter requirements for preventing overfishing, rebuilding overfished stocks, reducing bycatch, accounting for essential fish habitat, and assessing the impacts of regulations on coastal communities were now in place.[21]

The changes affecting groundfish fisheries in the 1990s include several not considered to fall within the "normal" types of fishery change. Stocks collapsed in New England and declined in the Pacific to levels requiring lower total allowable catch. The diversity of fishery interests expanded as environmental organizations and recreational fishing interests became more active in the council process. The level of public support for fisheries managed on a business-as-usual basis was very low, and the pressures for change were significant. The 1996 SFA introduced major change to the way management decision making was to be conducted. The SFA amended the MFCMA, renaming it the Magnuson-Stevens Fishery Conservation and Management Act (MSFCMA)

## Conclusion: Regional Adaptation and Management Resilience

The New England and Pacific regions experienced change throughout the postwar period. Changes before the passage of the FCMA were within what was considered normal. But the institutional changes represented by the FCMA and its successors, the MFCMA, the SFA, and the MSFCMA, were anomalous changes, as were the changes in public attitudes and values toward fisheries.

Management resilience in the two regions is due at least in part to three important regional attributes: the conditions at the point of implementation, the source of threats, and management styles.

## Initial Conditions

In New England, 1977 was a time of severe stock depletion on the heels of heavy foreign fishing. New entry into the fishery put further pressure on stocks. Interactions between the states were poorly coordinated, and the level of participation in management was weak. A prevailing ethic of strong individual autonomy precluded the adoption of a corporate model of decision making. The support of free competition on the ocean further retarded the adoption of output controls or entry controls. The council structure was kept rudimentary, and formal processes were kept to a minimum. The use of science in decision making was minimized.

In the Pacific, management intervention came at a time—1977—when there was a relative surplus in groundfish stocks that could temporarily absorb the increase in capacity. The region entered the new council system with a history of interstate coordination and the use of advisory groups in management. It adopted the corporate style of the MFCMA, taking full advantage of the enabling legislation to establish a diversified information and advisory system. The use of science in decision making was emphasized.

## Source of Threats

The source of a perceived threat, whether it is external or internal, determines whether there is a positive driving force that can create a common goal or a negative force that would preclude the formation of one. The impetus for the FCMA was the threat to U.S. fleets caused by foreign fishing, and the threat to U.S. fishery products by increased seafood imports. Both threats were external and resulted in collective support for the FCMA. But once the FCMA was passed, the nature of the threat changed. In New England it soon became clear that because stocks were overfished, what was allocated to one group of fishers would be at the expense of another. The threat was now internal. The issue became not "protect us from them" but rather "protect mine from you" (for example, Maine vs. Massachusetts, Gloucester vs. New Bedford). The focus on protecting what was considered to be "theirs" from other participants in the fishery kept the internal competition active and prevented formation of a common understanding or set of common objectives.

In the Pacific, because a surplus of stocks existed at the time the FCMA was implemented, there was some lead time before external threats became internal. As long as threats were considered to be external, people could concentrate on protecting insiders—they had the ability to learn about the fishery and to form common goals and objectives. However, once resources became more constrained, internal competition over allocations of fish introduced new strains into the management system.

## Management Styles

New England entered the council era with the traditional values of independence, autonomy, and apprehension about centralized government. The New England Fishery Management Council used the flexibility of the FCMA to avoid setting up the full corporate structure for decision making, choosing instead to proceed with minimal structures, ad hoc participation, and an unstructured and selective use of scientific information. Until the mid-1990s, the New England Fishery Management Council continued to rely on approaches to management better adapted to an earlier period of free competition than to the constraints of overcapitalization and resource scarcity.

The Pacific region, in contrast, went into the council system with a history of strong interstate coordination and industry participation in decision making, sliding more easily into the corporate structure. Human capital in participation, negotiation, and formal processes already existed to some extent and were further developed by the widespread use of advisory panels. Emphasis was placed on maintaining a structured council process. There was little public resistance to the idea that the federal government and the councils had a legitimate role in management.

The responses of the two regions and the resilience of their management to these sources of change have been quite different. New England fishery management has shown low levels of resilience to the changes this period has brought. The critical management functions of conservation and allocation have suffered, leaving the New England Fishery Management Council to cope with the legacy of poor adaptation to change. Pacific fishery management showed high levels of resilience to change until the late 1990s, when the accumulated stresses of overcapacity and the new requirements of the SFA were joined. The Pacific Fishery Management Council is now coping with these changes as it tries to create goals for the future. Will the New England patterns now emerge in the Pacific as resources decline, or will Pacific groundfish management remain resilient?

# Notes

1. National Marine Fisheries Service, 1998, *Report to Congress: Status of Fisheries of the United States,* October 1998.

2. S. Fordham, 1996, *New England Groundfish: From Glory to Grief* (Washington, D.C.: Center for Marine Conservation).

3. P. Shelley, J. Atkinson, E. Dorsey, and P. Brooks, 1996, The New England Fisheries: What Have We Learned? *Tulane Environmental Journal* 9(2): 221–244.

4. S. D. H. Wang and A. R. Rosenberg, 1997, U.S. New England Groundfish Management under the Magnuson-Stevens Conservation and Management Act, *Marine Resource Economics* 12: 361–366.

5. Pacific Fishery Management Council, 1998, *Status of the Pacific Coast Groundfish Fishery Through 1998 and Recommended Acceptable Biological Catches for 1999. Stock Assessment and Fishery Evaluation* (Portland, OR: Pacific Fishery Management Council).

6. Wang and Rosenberg 1997.

7. S. Hanna, 1998, Parallel Institutional Pathologies in Fisheries Management, pp. 25–35 in D. Symes, ed., *Northern Waters: Management Issues and Practice* (Oxford: Fishing News Books).

8. R. C. Hennemuth and S. Rockwell, 1987, History of Fisheries Conservation and Management, pp. 430–446 in R. H. Backus, ed., *Georges Bank* (Cambridge, MA: MIT Press).

9. Hennemuth and Rockwell 1987.

10. National Marine Fisheries Service, 1977, *Fisheries of the United States, 1976*, U.S. Department of Commerce, National Oceanic and Atmospheric Administration.

11. National Marine Fisheries Service 1977.

12. Hennemuth and Rockwell 1987.

13. W. G. Magnuson, 1968, The Opportunity Is Waiting…Make the Most of It, pp. 7–8 in D. Gilbert, ed., *The Future of the Fishing Industry of the United States,* New Series, Volume 4 (Seattle, WA: University of Washington Publications in Fisheries).

14. M. Hall-Arber and A. C. Finlayson, 1997, Role of Local Institutions in Groundfish Policy, pp. 111–140 in J. Boreman, B. S. Nakashima, J. A. Wilson, and R. L. Kendall, eds., *Northwest Atlantic Groundfish: Perspectives on a Fishery Collapse* (Bethesda, MD: American Fisheries Society).

15. Shelley, Atkinson, Dorsey, and Brooks 1996.

16. Shelley, Atkinson, Dorsey, and Brooks 1996.

17. New England Fishery Management Council, 1993, Amendment 5 to the Northeast Multispecies Fishery Management Plan Incorporating the Supplemental Environmental Impact Statement.

18. Pacific Fishery Management Council 1998.

19. S. Hanna, 1995, User Participation and Fishery Management Performance within the Pacific Fishery Management Council, *Ocean and Coastal Management* 28(1–3): 23–44.

20. National Marine Fisheries Service, 1998, *Fisheries of the United States, 1997,* U.S. Department of Commerce, National Oceanic and Atmospheric Administration.

21. National Oceanic and Atmospheric Administration, 1997, *A Guide to the SFA, Public Law 104–297* (Washington, D.C.: NOAA Office of General Counsel, U.S. Dept. of Commerce).

## CHAPTER 3

# The Economic Impacts of Reduced Marine Harvests on Regional Economies

*Laurie Houston, Rebecca Johnson,*
*Ed Waters, Hans Radtke, and John Gates*

## New England and Pacific Northwest Fishing Areas

The fishing industries in New England and the Pacific Northwest historically played a significant role in the early development of both these regions.[1] Today the fishing industries in these regions still play an important role in the U.S. fishing industry, and some coastal communities, but are relatively less important to the statewide economies. New England and the Pacific Northwest supply approximately 15 percent of the U.S. domestic commercial landings and 25 percent of the value of U.S. landings.[2]  Figure 1 depicts the fishing areas described in this paper. The New England area consists of Maine, New Hampshire, Massachusetts, Rhode Island, and Connecticut. The Northwest area consists of Oregon, Washington, and northern California. (When detailed data are not available for northern California from San Francisco to the northern border, we have used data for all of California.)

In an attempt to measure and compare the relative importance of the fishing industries to these areas, we have examined the changes in landings and value of landings in each area. Much of the decline in harvests in New England is the result of decreased groundfish stocks. In the Pacific Northwest, much of the decline is due to a decrease in salmon stocks in northern California and southern Oregon and to some extent the decrease in groundfish stocks. The focus of many government policies has been mostly on groundfish in New England and salmon in the Pacific Northwest. We discuss here some of the major government programs that have evolved to deal with the declining harvests, and the possible economic impact that reduced stocks and policy decisions may have on household income and federal, state, and local taxes.

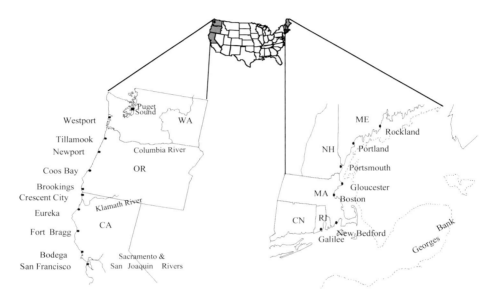

*Figure 1. Commercial fishing areas in New England and the Pacific Northwest.*

## Landing and Value Trends

In New England, landings were on a steady decline until the passing of the Magnuson-Stevens Fishery Conservation and Management Act in 1977 (figure 2). This act, which created the exclusive economic zone, virtually eliminated foreign fishing between 3 and 200 nautical miles from shore. The stated purpose of the act was to restore and conserve the fish. However, during this time local fishers were encouraged by government investment and loan programs to invest in expanding the local fishing fleets. Thus domestic fishing effort and landings increased and the fish stock began to decline again. Since the early 1980s total landings have been declining. The most recent increase in landings in the early 1990s is said by some researchers to be due mostly to increased fishing effort as fishers have been going farther away to fish.

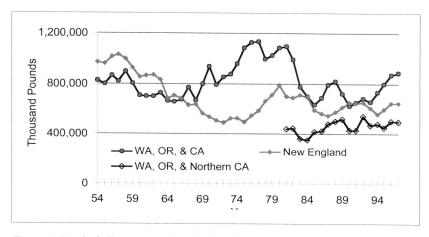

*Figure 2. Total of all commercial seafood landings in New England and the Pacific Northwest. Data sources:* Fishery Statistics of the United States, *U.S. Fish and Wildlife Service;* Fisheries of the United States Annual Reports, Current Fishery Statistics, *National Marine Fisheries Service; and PacFIN Database, September 1998 extraction, Pacific Fishery Management Council.*

In the Northwest, landings were not declining as dramatically as they were in New England before the Magnuson Act. Pacific ocean perch stocks were depleted in the late 1960s by foreign fishing, but other groundfish stocks were apparently healthy.[3] As in New England, by the 1980s many fisheries had reached or exceeded maximum sustainable production levels.[4] Landings in the Northwest were historically dominated by the salmon catch. However, in the early 1990s a new surimi processing industry dramatically increased the landings of Pacific whiting, primarily in Oregon. This accounts for much of the sharp rise in pounds landed in the Pacific Northwest region since 1991 (figure 2).

The major difference between the New England fishery and the Pacific Northwest fishery is the value of landings. The value of landings in New England, even after adjusting for inflation, increased sharply during the mid 1970s, leveled off in the 1980s, and has declined since 1991. The value of landings in the Pacific Northwest also increased throughout the 1960s and 1970s, but then fell dramatically in the early 1980s, had a small recovery in the late 1980s, and then declined sharply again (figure 3).

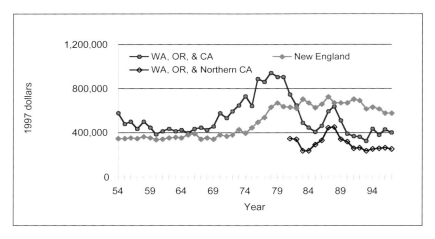

*Figure 3. Total value of all commercial seafood landings in New England and the Pacific Northwest. Data sources: Fishery Statistics of the United States, U.S. Fish and Wildlife Service; Fisheries of the United States Annual Reports, Current Fishery Statistics, National Marine Fisheries Service; and PacFIN Database, September 1998 extraction, Pacific Fishery Management Council.*

The relative stability of the value of landings in New England is due largely to a change in the species mix being harvested. As traditional groundfish species have declined, many fishers have augmented or replaced their groundfish catch with alternative species such as skates, sea urchins, and shrimp. In 1950, skates were not commercially harvested; in 1996 they represented 4.7 percent of total pounds landed.[5]   Many of these species also command a higher price per pound than the traditional groundfish. Thus even though landings have declined since 1980, the value of landings has remained relatively stable.

Until 1980, the average price per pound of landings in New England was similar to that in the Pacific Northwest. However, prices in the two regions then began to diverge, with the average price in New England increasing and the average price in the Pacific Northwest declining (figure 4). In 1954 the average price per pound (in 1997 dollars) of landings, after adjusting for inflation, was 70¢ per pound in the Pacific Northwest and 36¢ per pound in New England. In New England the average inflation adjusted price was as high as $1.33 per pound in 1987 but has de-

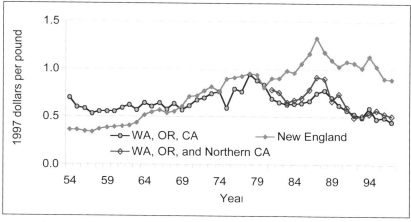

*Figure 4. Average price per pound of landings in New England and the Pacific Northwest. Data sources:* Fishery Statistics of the United States, *U.S. Fish and Wildlife Service;* Fisheries of the United States Annual Reports, Current Fishery Statistics, *National Marine Fisheries Service; and PacFIN Database, September 1998 extraction, Pacific Fishery Management Council.*

clined again to about 89¢ per pound in 1997. In the Pacific Northwest, the average inflation-adjusted price of all landings has declined to just 45¢ per pound from a high of 94¢ per pound in 1978. The decline in the value of landings in the Northwest is due in large part to the large proportion of lower-valued Pacific whiting being landed, a reduction of salmon landings, and lower salmon prices. Salmon prices have been declining over the past decade in response to increasing world supply of both farmed and wild salmon.[6]

## Species of Concern

The species of major concern in New England have been haddock, cod, and yellowtail flounder. The landings of haddock have dropped almost to zero, and those of flounder and cod have declined throughout the 1980s and 1990s, except for a couple of years in the late 1980s (figure 5). Some researchers speculate that the increase in the 1980s was most likely due to increased fishing effort as fishers went farther from port to fish. With Amendment 7 to the Northeast Multispecies Management Plan, fishers are being forced to reduce their fishing effort to just 88 days a year, and the Commerce Department is paying vessel owners to retire their vessels.[7]

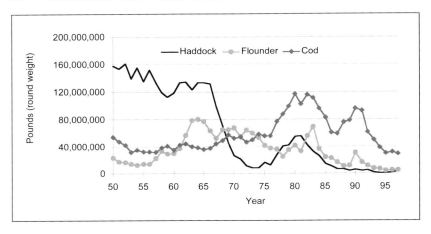

*Figure 5. Haddock, cod, and yellowtail flounder landings in New England.*
*Data source:* Commercial Fisheries Statistics, *Fisheries Statistics and Economics Division*

*Figure 6. Commercial coho and chinook landings in the Pacific Northwest. Data source: 50th Annual Report of the Pacific States Marine Fisheries Commission for the Year 1997.*

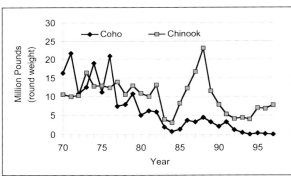

In the Northwest, the species of major concern have been salmon, especially coho and chinook. The combined commercial landings of coho salmon in California, Oregon, and Washington have dropped from an average of 15 million pounds in the early 1970s to almost zero in 1997 (figure 6). The combined commercial landings of chinook salmon in California, Oregon, and Washington have declined from a high of 23 million pounds in 1988 to a low of 4.4 million pounds in 1994. In the last three years landings have increased to about 7 million pounds but are still lower than average landings in the 1970s.

## Responses to the Decline in Fish Species

The two regions have responded similarly to the decline in fish species. Each region has regulated fishing effort by limiting the days at sea, establishing gear requirements, and closing or limiting access to fishing areas. Each has also closed certain fishing areas indefinitely to give the groundfish stocks in New England and salmon stocks in the Pacific Northwest a chance to recover. In the Pacific Northwest, they have also listed many coho and chinook salmon runs as threatened under the Endangered Species Act.

In April 1997 coho salmon of northern California and southern Oregon were listed as a threatened species.[8] In August 1998 coho along the central and northern Oregon coast were added to the threatened list.[9] In 1999, several chinook runs of salmon were also added. By March 1999 the chinook salmon runs of Puget Sound in Washington and those of the lower Columbia River in Washington and Oregon were listed as threatened. The spring run chinook of the upper Willamette in Oregon and the upper Columbia River in Washington were also listed.[10]

The decline of these fish populations led to disaster relief programs for ground fishers in New England and salmon fishers in the Pacific Northwest. Table 1 provides a partial list of recent programs that were set up in each region and the administrative agency involved.

## Employment Dependency

To compare the New England and Pacific Northwest fishing economies, we chose for analysis two smaller geographic regions representative of the fishing economies in each area (table 2). In the Northwest, coastal Oregon was chosen because it contains all of the major fishing sectors that exist in Washington, Oregon, and California, and it also has a major component of the new Pacific whiting industry. The coastal Oregon model includes all coastal counties, except for Lane and Douglas, which are mostly inland counties. In New England, where major population centers exist along the coast, it was difficult to choose a representative fishing community for which changes in the fishing sectors would not be washed out by the economic influences of metropolitan areas. We selected Bristol County, Massachusetts, to represent the New England area because it is the fishing community farthest away from a metropolitan area that also contains a large fishing community representing most of the fisheries in New England, such as the scallop, groundfish, and lobster fisheries.

*Table 1. Fishing Industry and fishery assistance programs in New England and the Northwest.*

| New England |
| --- |
| ◆ **Fishing Capacity Reduction Demonstration Program:** Groundfish Vessel Buyout (National Oceanic and Atmospheric Administration) |
| ◆ **Northeast Fishery Assistance Program: for the groundfish industry**<br>• <u>Revolving Loan Program:</u> Loans are made available to participants in the groundfishery to make improvements in existing businesses or to explore new businesses.<br>• (Economic Development Administration)<br>• <u>Direct Industry Assistance:</u><br>• National Marine Fisheries Service)<br> * *Fisheries Obligation Guarantee Program:* This program is designed to restructure existing debt.<br> * *Fishing Family Assistance Centers:* This program assisted fishing families in finding small business loans, workshops for profitable fishing business techniques, retraining programs, and various other assistance programs.<br> * *Fishing Industry Grants:* These grants are designed to promote the development of commercial fishing and markets for underexploited species, develop methods for eliminating or reducing bycatch, and create new business and alternative employment opportunities. |
| Pacific Northwest |
| ◆ **Northwest Emergency Assistance Program: for the salmon industry**<br>• <u>Habitat Restoration:</u> This section of the program hires fishers to plant trees, repair culverts, and undertake other watershed restoration activities.<br>• (Natural Resource Conservation Service)<br>• <u>Data Collection:</u> This section of the program hires fishers to collect data for salmon-related research projects such as stream spawning surveys, effectiveness of salmon hatcheries and net pens, and hooking mortality and encounter rates for commercial troll gear and sportfishing.<br>(Pacific States Marine Fisheries Commission)<br>• <u>License Buyout:</u> The buyout is aimed at reducing fishing effort on the stocks and to compensate commercial fishers for uninsured lost income.<br>(Washington Department of Fish and Wildlife) |
| ◆ **Oregon's coastal Salmon Restoration Initiative:** This program enlists the cooperation of private and public landowners to take part in stream restoration and monitoring. Initially aimed at the salmon fisheries of the coast range, it is being expanded throughout the state to include steelhead trout and other threatened species. (Oregon Governor's Watershed Enhancement Board and National Marine Fisheries Service) |

*Table 2. Fishing sectors for the coastal Oregon and Bristol County CGE models.*

| Coastal Oregon | Bristol County, MA |
|---|---|
| Groundfish trawlers | Class 2 scallop vessel |
| Shrimp and scallop draggers | Class 3 scallop vessel |
| Crab | Class 4 scallop vessel |
| Small boats | Class 2 groundfish trawler |
| Whiting | Class 3 groundfish trawler |
| | Southern inshore lobster fleet |
| | Northern inshore lobster fleet |

Note: There are also processing sectors for each of these fishing sectors.

Figure 7 shows industry groupings in terms of employment dependency. Employment dependency is defined as the jobs generated by the direct, indirect, and induced rounds of spending by each industry. Though the fishing sector in each area has a relatively small employment dependency (3 percent for Bristol County and 6 percent for coastal Oregon), it is still greater than most of the sectors that have been lumped together in the "other" category. Thus in each area the fishing sector is ranked approximately fifth, among all individual sectors, in terms of employment dependency.

The impact of industrialized metropolitan areas in New England is evident in these pie charts. In Bristol County, Massachusetts, 40 percent

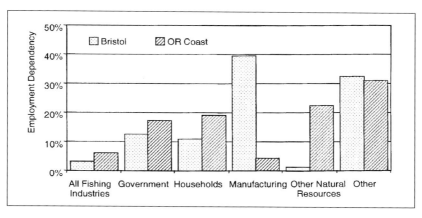

*Figure 7. Employment dependency in Bristol County, Massachusetts, and the Oregon coast. Data source: Minnesota IMPLAN Group, 1993 IMPLAN data.*

of the employment is dependent on the manufacturing sectors, compared to only 10 percent in coastal Oregon. Coastal Oregon on the other hand, is much more dependent on its natural resource-based industries. The natural resource-based industries, including fishing, represent 27 percent of the area's employment dependency. In comparison, natural resource-based industries in Bristol County, Massachusetts, represent only 5 percent of the area's employment dependency. This difference among coastal communities' dependency on fishing and other natural resource-based industries should be kept in mind when developing policy alternatives and evaluating their impact.

## Computable General Equilibrium Model

To determine the possible economic impact of reduced marine harvests on coastal communities, we used a computable general equilibrium model (CGE) rather than the standard input-output model. CGE models augment the basic interindustry relationships of the input-output model with explicit microeconomic-based behavior that captures the price responsiveness of producers, consumers, governments, enterprises, and other institutions. These aspects of the CGE model also enable one to look at the possible impacts of a wider range of alternative policy actions on regional economic variables, including output, employment, consumption, household income, and taxes.

The flexibility of CGE models allows the researcher to adopt more realistic behavioral assumptions regarding firms and households than characterize traditional models. A CGE model simulates an economy in which prices and quantities adjust to clear product and factor markets. It allows the substitution of factors to occur, and it allows some of these factors to move across firms and even out of the region. The model captures the optimizing behavior of producers and consumers and includes government as a major economic actor. All transactions are captured in a balanced, circular flow. CGE models can simulate external shocks to the local economy caused by changes in final demand, resource subsidies, or supply of public resources. They allow clear differentiation of market behavior that characterizes firms producing traded versus nontraded goods and services. Since CGE models incorporate the central behavioral assumptions of microeconomic theory, including the scarcity value of resources, they are well suited for the estimation of the impacts and net benefits of changes in public policies and thus provide generally more conservative and, it is hoped, more realistic results than a traditional input-output model.

# Model Scenarios

We used CGE models of coastal Oregon and Bristol County, Massachusetts, to demonstrate the economic impact of three possible scenarios, described below. The models were built using 1993 data from IMPLAN software.[11] We used regional fishing industry data from personal contacts within the industry to disaggregate the fishing sector into five separate fishing sectors for the Oregon coast model and seven sectors for the Bristol County model. This breakdown allowed us to look at possible implications for individual fishing sectors. We disaggregated the fish-processing sectors in the same manner, with a processing sector for each fishing sector. Data gathered through personal contacts suggested that each fishing sector in the Oregon coast also catches a small portion of groundfish along with its primary catch. Thus, while about 80 percent of the groundfish catch is harvested by groundfish trawlers, the remaining 20 percent is landed by boats primarily engaged in shrimp, scallop, salmon, whiting, or crab fisheries. An implication of this is that the impact of a decline in groundfish is spread across several fishing sectors. In the Bristol County model, on the other hand, each fishery is more specialized, resulting in a minimal amount of overlap among fishing fleets that, for modeling purposes, we assumed to be zero.

For comparison purposes, we chose three scenarios involving groundfish to represent possible economic impacts of reduced marine harvests. Each scenario represents an approximate 20 percent reduction in groundfish revenues. These scenarios assume a short-run response, and as such it is assumed that the processors will not augment their local supply with imports.

## Scenario 1

Scenario 1 assumes there is a 20 percent reduction in groundfish catch because the fishery has become less productive. This is the situation that the New England fishery has experienced in the traditional groundfish industry and the Pacific Northwest is just beginning to experience. In this scenario the boats spend just as much time and effort fishing but catch fewer groundfish. The producers reduce their purchases and output accordingly.

## Scenario 2

Scenario 2 models a 27 percent reduction in the groundfish trawl fleet equivalent to a 20 percent reduction in groundfish revenues. This results in a $6 million reduction in groundfish revenues in the Oregon coast model and a $14 million reduction in the Bristol County model. As compensation for taking their boats out of the groundfish fleet, Oregon trawl boat owners are paid $6 million. Bristol County owners are paid $14 million. Buyback proceeds were distributed to households in proportion to the baseline SAM distribution of proprietor's income from 1993 IMPLAN data.

It is assumed that the buyback money comes from the federal government or some other source outside the local economy. The processors adjust purchases and output accordingly, and other fishing sectors in the Oregon coast model are allowed to pick up some of the slack from the other fish that the trawlers used to catch, but they are not allowed to increase their groundfish catch. For example, the crabbers will be able to increase their crab harvests by the amount of crab that the trawl boats used to harvest. In the Bristol County model, the lobster and scallop sectors are assumed to harvest little or no groundfish.

## Scenario 3

Scenario 3 is set up exactly like scenario 2, but the households are not compensated for the removal of groundfish trawl boats. Processors adjust purchases and output accordingly, and other sectors are again allowed to pick up some of the slack in the Oregon coast model, but not in the Bristol County model.

# Impacts

## Household Income

The impact on each region's household income associated with each scenario is illustrated in figure 8. The change in household income is divided into low-, medium-, and high-income levels. Low household income is between $0 and $20,000 a year, medium is from greater than $20,000 to $50,000 a year, and high is greater than $50,000 a year. In each region, the percent change in household income is never much more than 0.2 percent. This may seem like an insignificant change, but keep in mind that the model examines the impact of a change in only one portion of the overall fishing industry, and the fishing industry represents between 3 percent and 6 percent of each region's total economy. Thus it is more

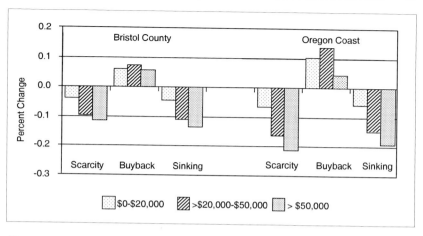

*Figure 8. Percent change in household income.*

important to look at the relative changes among regions and income levels than the absolute change.

Scenarios 1 and 3 represent the groundfish scarcity and the trawl boat sinking scenarios. Each scenario results in a negative impact on all household income levels in both regions. The high-income households experience the greatest percent decrease in income. In the Bristol County model, the impact on high-income households is 3 times as great as the impact on low-income households. In the Oregon coast model, the impact on high-income households is 3.5 times greater than the impact on low-income households.

Scenario 2, the buyback, is the only scenario with a positive impact on household income. This is because the money used to purchase the trawlers came from outside the local economy. This influx of money from outside the local economy more than offsets the negative impact of a 20 percent reduction in groundfish revenues. The percent increase in household income is split relatively evenly among household income levels in the Bristol County model. In the coastal Oregon model, however, the low- and medium-household income groups experience a relatively larger percent increase in income than the high-income group experiences. In both models, the middle-income group ($20,000–$50,000) is expected to gain the most from the buyback policy.

In all scenarios, the impact is greater for the coastal Oregon model because the coastal Oregon community is more dependent on the fishing industry than is the Bristol County community. In both regions the low-income households are slightly better off under the scarcity scenario than the sinking scenario. The medium income households in both regions benefit most from the buyback scenario.

## Industry and Household Taxes

Another way to look at the impact of these scenarios is to look at the changes in taxes. When making policy decisions it may be helpful to look at the impacts of changes in taxes from three different facets. Policymakers may want to know how a policy decision will change industrial taxes either at the federal or state and local level. They may also want to know how a decision may affect household taxes at either the federal or state and local level. Last, they may want to know what the net impact is to government revenues caused by changes in industrial and household income levels.

In each region, all three scenarios have a negative impact on industrial taxes, both at the federal level and at the state and local level. The impact on taxes will obviously depend largely on the tax structure of a given state or local municipality. In this paper we do not get into the nuances of local tax structures, except to say that federal policy decisions may have drastically different impacts on individual communities, depending on their local tax structures. For example, in the Oregon coast model, there is a larger impact on federal taxes than on state and local taxes. However, in the Bristol County model, the percent change in industrial taxes is the same for federal taxes as it is for state and local taxes (figure 9). Thus in all

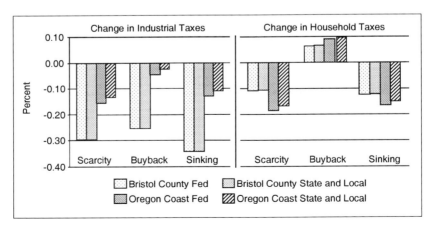

*Figure 9. Percent change in industrial and household taxes.*

three scenarios, the impact on local tax revenues from industry is greater for the Bristol County area than the coastal Oregon area.

Another difference between the two regions is the magnitude of the impact. In all three scenarios, the percent decrease in industrial taxes is much larger in the Bristol County model than in the Oregon coast model. In the scarcity scenario, the percent decrease in industrial taxes for the Bristol County model is about twice as great as the percent decrease in the coastal Oregon model. In the trawl boat buyback scenario, the percent change in the Bristol County model is about six times as great, and in the trawl boat sinking scenario it is about three times as great.

When we compare the differences in household taxes between the two regions, the result is a little different. The scarcity and trawl boat sinking scenarios both have negative impacts on household taxes. However, the trawl boat buyback scenario has a positive impact because boat owners are compensated for removing their boats from the fishery (figure 9). Even though more boats are removed from the Bristol fishery, the percent change in household taxes is smaller in the Bristol County model than in the Oregon coast model because the fishing industry makes up a smaller proportion of the Bristol economy than of the Oregon coast economy. It is interesting to note that in the Oregon coast model, the percent change in household taxes is greater than the percent change in industrial taxes (for all scenarios) but the opposite is true for the Bristol County model. In the Bristol County model, the percent change in household taxes is much smaller than the percent change in industrial taxes. However, the disparity between the two regions is much smaller when we look at the percent change in household taxes than it is when we look at the percent change in industrial taxes.

When we examine the net impact of these changes on government revenues, the groundfish scarcity scenario results in almost exactly the same percent decrease in government revenues for each region (figure 10). This similarity implies that the relatively smaller impact on household taxes in the Bristol County model partially offsets the large impact on industrial taxes. In the trawl boat buyback scenario, the net impact is negative for Bristol County and positive for coastal Oregon. In the Bristol County model, the positive impact from the change in household taxes is outweighed by the negative impact on industrial taxes. In the coastal Oregon model, the negative impact on industrial taxes is outweighed by the positive impact on household taxes. In the trawl boat sinking scenario, the negative percent change in government revenues for the Bristol

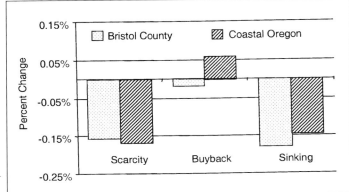

*Figure 10. Net percent change in government revenues.*

County model is slightly larger than it is for the coastal Oregon model. Thus in terms of tax revenues, the scarcity scenario is the least desirable scenario for coastal Oregon, and the trawl boat sinking scenario is the least desirable for Bristol County.

## Summary

The fishing industry in New England and the Pacific Northwest is important to the coastal economies of each region, though the economy in the Bristol County area appears to be more diversified and less dependent on fishing than the Oregon coast economy. The Pacific Northwest has been concerned for many years about the decline in many salmon stocks and recently also has been experiencing what many biologists believe to be a decline in groundfish stocks. The New England fishery has been concerned with declining groundfish stocks for many years. In response to adverse fishery conditions, both regions have implemented various programs aimed at helping the fisheries and the economies associated with the fisheries.

Because the two regions have experienced similar conditions in their fisheries but have dissimilar economic structures, they provided an excellent opportunity to compare the impacts that identical fishery policies may have on areas with different economic structures. The most notable difference between these two economies is in their employment dependency. Bristol County relies much more on manufacturing sectors than does the Oregon coast, and the Oregon coast depends much more on fishery and other natural resources. For purposes of comparison, we modeled three scenarios of reduced groundfish harvests in the two regions.

Scenario 1 was designed to model the impact of a general decline in the availability of groundfish in both the New England and Northwest regions. Scenarios 2 and 3 were designed to model the impact of two policy alternatives for reducing the groundfish fleet.

One of the major differences between the two regions is the impact on household income. In all three scenarios, the decrease in groundfish output has a greater impact on household income in the Oregon coast model than in the Bristol County model. This is most likely due to the differing dependence each region has on fishing. Even though the Bristol fishing sector is bigger than Oregon's, the Oregon coast is more dependent on fishing and so is more affected by changes in that sector than is the Bristol area.

The other striking dissimilarity between the two model outcomes is the change in industrial taxes. In all scenarios, the Bristol County model results in much larger decreases in industrial taxes than the Oregon coast model. The difference between the two areas is much smaller with respect to the change in household taxes, and the percent change is greater in the Oregon coast model than in the Bristol County model. The biggest difference in the tax structures between these two regions is that Oregon does not have a sales tax and Massachusetts does. There may also be other nuances of each state's tax structures that contribute to this difference.

Thus when policymakers are designing national fishery policies, there are several things they should consider that will affect regional economies. It is important for regulators to determine how dependent an area is on the fishing industry because this dependence will play a role in how well fishers are able to adjust to the policy. Policymakers should also have an idea about how the policy will affect various income level groups and in turn how this change in income will affect industrial and household taxes. The tax issue will be of special concern if the regional tax revenues are highly dependent on either industrial or household taxes. Finally comes the issue of equity. A CGE model similar to the ones built for the Oregon coast model and the Bristol County model can help policymakers determine some of the possible impacts of their decisions. This knowledge should help them make more informed decisions regarding issues of regional equity.

## Notes

1. Raymond McFarland, 1911, *A History of the New England Fisheries* (Philadelphia: University of Pennsylvania); Anthony Netboy, 1974, *The Salmon: Their*

*Fight for Survival* (Boston: Houghton Mifflin); and Anthony Netboy, 1980, *The World's Most Harassed Fish* (London: A. Deutsch).

2. National Marine Fisheries Service, 1997, *Current Fishery Statistics.*

3. Pacific Fishery Management Council (PFMC), *Status of the Pacific Coast Groundfish Fishery,* September 1996.

4. PFMC, September 1996.

5. These landing statistics are derived from data supplied by the National Marine Fisheries Service, Fisheries Statistics and Economic Division.

6. University of Alaska Seafood Market Information Service, 1998.

7. National Oceanic and Atmospheric Administration, "Recovery Measures fro New England Groundfish Approved; New Fishing Rules Begin in July—$25M Vessel Buyout to Follow," press release no. 96-R139, May 16, 1996.

8. National Oceanic and Atmospheric Administration, "Federal Fisheries Agency's New Rule Protecting West Coast Coho Takes Advantage of State Conservation Efforts," press release no. 97-R150, July 15, 1997.

9. *Federal Register* 63, no. 153 (10 August 1998).

10. *Federal Register* 64, no. 56 (24 March 1999).

11. Minnesota IMPLAN Group, 1996, IMPLAN Professional Software, Stillwater, MN (1993 data for Bristol County, MA, and coastal counties in Oregon).

# Communities

# CHAPTER 4

# Who Talks the Talk? The Voice of Community in Two New England Fishing Ports

*Madeleine Hall-Arber*

## Introduction

**Community** (kə-myoo′ ni-te) n., pl. –ties. **1.a.** A group of people living in the same locality and under the same government. . . . . **2.** A group of people having common interests. . . . . **5.** *Ecol.* a. A group of plants and animals living and interacting with one another in a specific region under relatively similar environmental conditions. (*American Heritage College Dictionary,* 1993)

Community has probably always played a role in resilience and change in the New England groundfish fisheries. Fishing, as an industry, fosters the development of community in the second sense, "people having common interests." However, fishing, as an occupation, also appeals to competitive individuals who voice a desire for "independence."[1] These norms suggest that common interests or goals could be difficult to identify. Furthermore, immigrant populations with fishing traditions settled in several areas in New England, creating ethnic communities within larger fishing-dependent port communities. This strengthened the social bonds among some fishing groups but created less homogenous conditions in some places.

Social scientists recognize the potential significance of community in fisheries management, suggesting that successful fisheries management is more likely to be achieved with the participation of community members.[2] McCay and Jentoft suggest that failures associated with fisheries management may reflect a community rather than market failure.[3] However, Davis and Bailey warn that a high degree of organizational and structural variation exists at the local level concomitant with wide differences in the understanding of what "community" means.[4] In particular, they note that the existence and position of local elites can significantly alter the development of management strategies.

Recently, the importance of sustaining fisheries communities has taken on the force of law with the passage of the Magnuson-Stevens Fishery Conservation and Management Act of 1996, also referred to as the Sustainable Fisheries Act. The act requires fishery management measures to

> take into account the importance of fishery resources to fishing communities in order to (A) allow the sustained participation of such communities, and (B) to the extent practicable, minimize adverse economic impacts on such communities (M-SFCMA, 16 U.S.C. §1851).

The definition of a *fishing* community has now been codified as

> a community which is substantially dependent on or substantially engaged in the harvest or processing of fishery resources to meet social and economic needs, and includes fishing vessel owners, operators and crew, and United States fish processors that are based in such a community (M-SFCMA, 16 U.S.C. §1802).

Although it need not necessarily be an incorporated entity, the act does require that a community be a "specific location."

Gloucester and New Bedford have long been two of the most significant groundfish ports in the Northeast region of the U.S. For years, both figured prominently in the annually published National Marine Fisheries Service (NMFS) document *Fisheries of the United States*. New Bedford was typically among the top 10 ports landing the highest value of product, and Gloucester was among those ports landing the largest volume of fish. Each of these cities' well-developed fishing industries has led to an extensive network of fisheries-dependent businesses—all of which are affected by changes in fisheries.

In this paper, I explore the similarities and differences between the organizational response to change in the two ports, identifying some of the key variables leading to the different responses. I suggest some reasons Gloucester functions more successfully as a fishing community than does New Bedford. Finally, I use a recent case history to raise issues related to the representation of communities. It demonstrates that the underlying question, Who speaks for the community?—so crucial for effective management—may easily be answered incorrectly.

## Community, Organizations, and Management

Studies of successful natural resource co-management draw attention to the fact that homogeneous communities tend to be more successful than heterogeneous ones.[5] In consequence, to achieve homogeneity, some have considered defining community as based on gear type, vessel size, fishery style, and so on, instead of geography. Nadel-Klein and Davis, for example, talk about fishing groups as "occupational communities."[6] Similarly, elsewhere in this collection, Conway refers to "communities of interest."

Since there are fisheries organizations that are not dependent on geographic setting, based instead on gear type, one could reasonably ask if these groupings could appropriately be considered communities of interest. I suggest that the terms "organization" and "community" both imply that the group so defined has a sense of identity, that its participants share some values and therefore can work toward agreed upon goals and objectives, but that the term "community" implies more complexity than the term "organization." The complexity lies in the variety of occupations or functions served by individuals in the community, so that one would have an organization of harvesters, for example, but a community of fishing industry participants that would include harvesters, processors, fuel dealers, marina owners, and so on. With the complexity comes the difficulty of incorporating "community" into the management process. Again, the question arises, Who speaks for the community?

Pinkerton notes that it is organized interests who are likely to be recognized as legitimate stakeholders for management purposes.[7] Organizations also avoid some of the complications associated with defining community since individuals who have joined an organization are self-selecting and apparently support the primary positions of the organization. The management regime in the Northeast U.S. implicitly recognizes organizations. It is the leaders of organizations who are appointed to the management council and to advisory boards. The question remains, however, What makes a group of organizations coalesce into a community? And, if a community is formed, does it properly have only one voice? If not one, then what combination of organizations can properly represent the community? I turn now to Gloucester and New Bedford to explore these ideas.

## Gloucester's Organizations

With regard to the fishing industry, Gloucester is by far the better organized of the two ports. It also has a much stronger sense of itself as a fishing community. The Gloucester Fishermen's Wives Association (GFWA), founded in 1969, actively represents the industry at Fishery Management Council meetings, fights oil drilling on Georges Bank, promotes underutilized seafood, and so on. In 1994, anticipating the need for building consensus in Gloucester about how the industry properly fits in the town's future, GFWA hosted a series of meetings entitled "Vision 2020." This effort brought together a wide array of individuals and representatives of organizations and institutions from all sectors of the town. Goals and objectives were formulated during a lengthy process. Many of them provide an ongoing sense of direction to the activities of various organizations in the town.

Gloucester also supports the Gloucester Fisheries Commission, a town board established by the city council in 1956, composed of the mayor, three city council members, and five members of the fishing industry. In addition to the mayor, local and regional politicians are active supporters of the fishing industry.

Greenpeace, an environmental organization, opened an office in Gloucester with a representative who has established herself as a voice of reason and concern, championing fishers and the fishing community. Wellspring House is a social service agency that has worked closely with the GFWA to facilitate meetings, particularly during the Vision 2020 process. Those associated with the agency are very concerned about maintaining a livable town. The minister for the Unitarian-Universalist Church has also played a role in meeting facilitation.

## New Bedford's Organizations

New Bedford, on the other hand, lacks a leading organization in the fishing industry—though there has been some jockeying for a leadership role among various groups. When major changes to the Multispecies Fisheries Management Plan (the plan pertaining to the key groundfish species) were being reviewed at public hearings, many of the fishing industry speakers addressed the council as individuals, captains, or crew of draggers. At that time, the Offshore Mariners Association had the broadest membership base because it included both draggers and scallopers. The organization has since disbanded. The Seafarers Union occasionally represents fishing crew members at public hearings.

The New Bedford Seafood Coalition may have replaced the Offshore Mariners as the organization with the broadest membership base. In August 1997 its executive director was named to the New England Fishery Management Council. Rarely, however, is the coalition noted by fishers as the appropriate representative of the city's fishing industry. The Greater New Bedford Fishermen's Family Emergency Center hired a fisherman/boat owner as an outreach specialist who has been an articulate spokesman for portions of the industry at council meetings and hearings but does not purport to represent anyone else's view but his own.

### Women's Organizations

Before 1969, the Fishermen's Wives Association, predominantly Newfoundland fishermen's wives, was an active group. For a time, the Offshore Mariners Wives Association gained prominence but has diminished to only a small handful of women who organize the annual Blessing of the Fleet.

A relatively new organization, Shore Support, has gained the backing of the New Bedford Working Capital Network. In contrast to previous wives' groups in New Bedford, Shore Support has made outreach to the Portuguese-speaking portion of the industry a high priority. Modeling itself after the Gloucester Fishermen's Wives Association, Shore Support helped conduct a needs survey of members of the fishing industry and community. In addition, it has a cable television program and has submitted an innovative proposal for aquaculture and hydroponics to Saltonstall-Kennedy for funding. If Shore Support is as successful as the GFWA in attracting and engaging diverse interests, it may eventually become a leading organization in New Bedford.

### Politicians

Representative Barney Frank of the U.S. House replaced Gerry Studds as the most active political leader for the New Bedford fishing industry. Few of the local political leaders or state representatives have consistently taken an active interest in the New Bedford industry. The politicians representing Gloucester, on the other hand, are quite vocal in their concerns about the fisheries and often support programs geared toward the industry.

# Contrasts in Community-Building
# and Talking the Talk

Both New Bedford and Gloucester have active fishing communities, and a variety of organizations associated with the industry play roles in fisheries management. As the search for more effective management considers co-management as an alternative strategy, community takes on added value in the fisheries context. But communities are not uniform in their ability to form cohesive policies or speak with a unified voice. New Bedford's fishing community has been less able than Gloucester's to find its voice.

## Economic Context

Gloucester has been considered an important fishing port for over 350 years. The symbol of Gloucester is its statue of the Man at the Wheel. Fishing dominates both the community's self image and tourism promotion. Gloucester also serves as a bedroom community for Boston and in recent years has been successful in attracting light industry, so it has not failed to diversify. Nevertheless, fishing and related businesses still dominate. Despite the economic difficulties associated with the fisheries, Gloucester gives the impression of optimism toward the future with several fisheries-related construction projects and other development.

New Bedford, in contrast, has gone through several boom and bust cycles: whaling and shipbuilding dominated the city's economy in the early and mid-1800s, followed by textiles. Glass and metalwork, golf balls and film (Polaroid) were important manufacturing products until very recently. When New Bedford was the top dollar port, fishing was also considered an extremely important part of the city's economy. But fishing has also been associated with negative images of alcoholism, drug use, and AIDS. Derelict boats and salvaged parts dot the wharves; boarded buildings and a quiet downtown lend the city an air of waiting. Until recently, the only large-scale development proposed for the city was a casino to be built away from the harbor. There are indications, however, that New Bedford's waterfront will again move out of its depression. Plans for a state-of-the art aquarium have been developed and fundraising has successfully begun. What the implications are for the fishing industry is yet to be determined.

## The Strike

The event perhaps most devastating to New Bedford's organizations and sense of community was a fishers' strike. Unlike Gloucester fishers, most New Bedford fishing crew members, especially on scallopers, were unionized, represented by the Seafarer's Union. In the 1970s, vessel owners succeeded in breaking the union. The bitterness of the struggle, though, left divisiveness in the fishing community that has not yet been overcome.

## Geography

Proximity to the New England Regional Fishery Management Council meetings eases the burden of participation for Gloucester residents. GFWA always sends a representative or two to council and committee meetings and almost always offers a position statement during public comment periods. Because the majority of the meetings are held 15 minutes from Gloucester, GFWA can muster groups of fishers even at the last minute. New Bedford, however, is about a two-hour drive in reasonable traffic and weather, so though various organizations each send a representative, seldom are groups of fishers able to attend. Without the experience of observing the various representatives at work, the members are less likely to see their value or rally behind one organization as the lead.

## Other Factors

Other factors constraining the development of a unified voice or a leading organization among the fishers of New Bedford include the effects of ethnicity, for example, language barriers and a limited public role for women. Furthermore, a belief among many of the immigrants that they will be returning to their country of origin dampens some of their commitment to their "temporary" home. In addition, no leader with sufficient charisma to mobilize disparate interest groups has arisen in New Bedford.[8]

# Whose Voice? A Cautionary Tale

The foregoing describes differences in the development of a unified voice for each of the two dominant fishing communities in New England. In this section, I present a case study that draws attention to the conflicts within one of these communities. It should serve as a cautionary tale to managers who think it is sufficient to have representatives of selected organizations participate in management discussions. Although Gloucester's fishing industry is clearly well organized and even has a "leading" organization, consideration of events in 1997 suggests that only open dialogue and opportunities for everyone to offer input will lead to properly represented communities.

In September 1996, it appeared that Gloucester was going to jump-start their flagging fishing industry by unprecedented unified action, leading to resurgence in the herring industry. An organization, the Gloucester Herring Corporation, was formed of 11 prominent businesses and nonprofits that included several processors, a shipper, an ice company, two cold storage companies, an oil service, and the GFWA. The group planned to take a multifaceted approach to harvest; process, pack, and ship herring for the export market; and seek new preparations of herring that would eventually lead to growth in a domestic market. Their enthusiasm was contagious and the corporation won a $400,000 grant from the U.S. Economic Development Agency to analyze the Northeast herring product and its potential as a development opportunity for Gloucester. GFWA also won a smaller grant from NMFS' Saltonstall-Kennedy Program to develop new herring recipes and give cooking demonstrations in area supermarkets.

There was historical precedent for Gloucester's interest in herring. From 1961 to 1966 the USSR landed Georges Bank herring in quantities ranging from 38,000 metric tons to 150,000 metric tons. In 1967 Poland and the German Democratic Republic joined the Soviets, and over the course of the decade, nine other countries, including the U.S. with Gloucester vessels, took up the chase for herring. But the heavy fishing pressure took its toll and the stock collapsed. For 15 years no commercial landings of herring were reported from Georges Bank. Recent assessments, however, indicate that the Georges Bank herring stock has finally recovered. Canada conservatively estimates a spawning biomass of 100,000 to 200,000 metric tons, whereas the U.S. estimates are considerably higher. The Gloucester Herring Corporation wanted to make sure Gloucester could successfully return to a focus on herring.

By late March of 1997, however, disenchantment fractured the Gloucester Herring Corporation. Competing visions of what is right and good for the East Coast fishing industry clashed over the Gloucester Herring Corporation's proposal to build a $10 million plant on the Jodfrey State Fish Pier and to bring in a 369-foot factory trawler, *Atlantic Star,* to fish for herring and mackerel.

The most vocal proponents of the plant and factory trawler were Mayor Bruce Tobey; Vito Calomo, executive director of the Gloucester Fisheries Commission; and Frank Elliott, owner of Elliott Shipping Company, with his assistant Bob Blair—that is, the leading local politician, the nominal voice of the fishing industry, and a leading businessman. In theory, these "local elites" should have provided a representative view of the community. But, as it turns out, they did not represent the views of the majority of the town.

A series of public meetings was called by a grassroots organization, Gloucester Initiatives, formed specifically to oppose what it viewed as a threat to the "real" fishing community. Over 200 people gathered on short notice to hear the proponents of the project present their proposal and rationale. What the proponents thought they presented was a proposal that showed benefits to the community of Gloucester through a plan that would exploit the reported abundance of herring modeled on techniques used for exploitation of pelagic species in Europe. The proponents particularly touted the creation of a plant and the jobs that would be created.

But when fishers learned that 98 percent of the Gloucester Herring Corporation was to be owned by the Dutch company Parlevict and Van Der Plas, they were sharply disappointed. In addition, the specter was raised of the return of foreign fleets to Georges Bank, albeit under the guise of a U.S.-built incinerator boat converted by the Norwegians to factory trawling. Other Gloucester residents questioned the ability of the herring stocks to support the proposed quantities of harvesting. The number of jobs claimed for a plant that was primarily focused on packing and freezing was also questioned. Still others pointed out that even if Gloucester fishers were offered jobs on the factory trawler, few would be interested. The usual multimonth fishing schedules of factory trawlers would not fit the norms and values of the many Gloucester fishers who are family oriented.

Opponents of the project also strongly opposed allocating the only remaining undeveloped parcels of land at the State Fish Pier for a private, Dutch-owned concern instead of for a proper public use. Specifically, it would preclude use of the parcels for a "stalls building," a new business incubator facility, and an innovation center that could be used to help diversify the Gloucester fishing industry into new value-added markets.

Eventually, the Gloucester Herring Corporation withdrew its proposal. Mayor Tobey called on selected residents to attend closed-door hearings to develop consensus on what should follow. Reportedly, the consensus goal of the group is to identify funding for upgrading Gloucester plants and boats (and thus improve the quality of herring product) and for marketing analysis to determine how best to sell herring. But the closed-door policy for the "round table discussion" did not earn points for the mayor. Several people who were not included in the discussion expressed the fear that Tobey was "stacking the deck against the opponents to the factory trawler and plant" and that "the last has not been heard on the topic." After a few weeks, two or three concerned citizens who had not been invited to the roundtable appeared at the meeting hall and refused to leave. The mayor backed down on the closed-door policy and eventually became much more conciliatory.

## Conclusion

The project described collapsed because the residents of Gloucester failed to rally behind it. The design of the project appeared to contradict some of the norms of Gloucester's fishing community. Stratification in the community would have increased had the project been implemented. In particular, the local elite would have reaped advantages that would have been denied others in the industry.

The controversy generated sufficient publicity to draw the attention of other fishing communities in the Northeast region of the U.S. and Canada. No other port has agreed to allow the *Atlantic Star* to use their facilities as a home port. The proponents were blindsided by the opposition, and their backers could lose millions of dollars if a home is not found for the factory trawler. The opponents to the project have breathed a sigh of relief that the factory trawler and plant will not be calling Gloucester home. However, they are disappointed that a project that started out as inclusive, egalitarian, and visionary became a threat to the way of life they had hoped would be renewed.

## What Can We Learn from This Case?

First, the herring development issue emphasizes the importance of open meetings to educate those involved, elicit different points of view, elucidate the details, and develop consensus. Second, the positions of titular public servants and local elites cannot be taken as gospel: they do not always and everywhere speak for the community. So, again I ask, Who does speak for the community?

There is no easy or quick answer. It is obvious that a fishing community, whether defined by the dictionary or Magnuson-Stevens, is not a homogeneous entity. But as others have noted, examination of social organization and socioeconomic dynamics is the strength of social science research.[9] Fishery managers should demand ongoing support of professional social science research. In addition, the outreach and extension programs of many universities, nongovernment organizations (for example, environmental groups), and welfare and advocacy groups can provide knowledgeable observations about fishing communities. Managers should talk to a wide range of organizations, even those only peripherally involved in areas of related interests. They should talk to individuals, as well as organization heads. If a community is contemplating an expensive or extensive project, focus groups can be used effectively to identify likely points of contention. Unfortunately, the techniques that could lead to avoiding similar events in the future are counterintuitive to most businesses. Trade secrets, proprietary information, and competition, rather than cooperation and open discussion, are often regarded as requisites in the competitive business culture.

## Notes

1. John Poggie, Jr., and Richard Pollnac, 1978, *Social Desirability of Work and Management Among Fishermen in Two New England Ports*, Anthropological Working Paper No. 5. (Kingston, RI: International Center for Marine Resource Development); John B. Gatewood and Bonnie McCay, 1990, Comparison of Job Satisfaction in Six New Jersey Fisheries: Implications for Management, *Human Organization* 49(1): 14–25; Marian Binkley, 1995, *Risks, Dangers, and Rewards in the Nova Scotia Offshore Fishery* (Montreal: McGill-Queen's University Press).

2. Elinor Pinkerton, 1989, Attaining Better Fisheries Management Through Co-Management: Prospects, Problems, and Propositions, in E. Pinkerton, ed., *Co-operative Management of Local Fisheries: New Directions for Improving Management and Community Development* (Vancouver: University of British Columbia Press).

3. Bonnie McCay and Svein Jentoft, 1998, Market or Community Failure? Critical Perspectives on Common Property Research, *Human Organization* 57(1): 21–29.

4. Anthony Davis and Connor Bailey, 1996, Common in Custom, Uncommon in Advantage: Common Property, Local Elites and Alternative Approaches to Fisheries Management, *Society and Natural Resources* 9(3): 251–266.

5. Pinkerton 1989; Elinor Ostrom, 1990, *Governing the Commons* (Cambridge: Cambridge University Press).

6. Jane Nadel-Klein and Dona Lee Davis, 1988, Introduction, in *To Work and To Weep: Women in Fishing Economies*, Social and Economic Papers No. 18, Institute of Social and Economic Research (Newfoundland: Memorial University of Newfoundland).

7. Pinkerton 1989.

8. Madeleine Hall-Arber, 1996, Hear Me Speak: Italian and Portuguese Women Facing Fisheries Management, *Anthropologica* 38: 221–248.

9. Davis and Bailey 1996.

# CHAPTER 5

# Community Infrastructure and the Development of Human Capital: A Pacific View

*Lori A. Cramer*

## Background

Over the past 30 years, fishing organizations and industries have been the subject of many studies. Traditionally, when rural fishing communities have been studied, economic factors have been the primary focus of scientific investigations. Today, social scientists recognize that noneconomic factors must also be considered in order to gain a more complete understanding of the social impacts of change.[1] Some of the noneconomic factors include fishers' attitudes (toward government, agencies, environmentalists, and so on), impacts of technological change, cultural dimensions of fisher groups, and demographic shifts in fisher populations.

Although social science is concerned with the relationship between community viability and resource dependence, few studies explicitly explore how fishing families and groups also influence (and are influenced by) their residential community infrastructure. What needs clarification is how fishing livelihoods are rooted in the residential community. This missing connection between people who fish and the community in which they live has important implications for understanding the social impact of fishing policy. As it stands, "the logic and dynamics of [current] management policies give little recognition to the fact that for many in small community settings fishing and ocean resources are as much expressions of social relations between kin and familiars, as they are about economics and property."[2]

## The Role of the Residential Community

The need to better understand the link between fishing livelihoods and residential communities was reiterated in the 1996 revision of the Magnuson-Stevens Fishery Conservation and Management Act. This document indicates that the impact of policy on human communities needs to be considered as part of future policy decisions. As social scientists have pointed out, identity is rooted not only in our "way of life" or occupations, but also in a place or community. The word "community" can take on many connotations, depending on the discipline and scale of investigation.[3] For this paper, "fishing community" refers to the occupationally defined group associated with commercial fishing; "residential community" is the town or city where people live. The residential communities described here are natural resource-based communities where people's social and cultural identities are intertwined with the production of a natural resource.

As members of a residential community, fishers and fishing families are one of many groups of people making up the local community. Given the tie to place, there is likely to be a symbiotic relationship between commercial fishers and nonfishers within a given residential community. Not only is the residential community socially important to the fishers and their families, but it may be the case that a commercial fishing heritage provides a backdrop with which nonfishers also identify (for example, nonfishers may feel a sense of pride or identity being from a fishing community). In addition to a common identity with place, issues of integration into the community are tied to occupational positions. Occupational and economic positions within the community provide the structural base for the broader political and social class system.[4] Therefore, occupational integration serves as a structural link to a common identity of place.

Understanding the context of the residential community provides insight into current issues of community cohesion. Competing interests across social groups in the direction of future community goals may exacerbate long-standing community conflict over nonfishing issues (for example, the funding of school bonds or the location of new businesses). Such sentiments might transfer into negative attitudes about the current needs of the fishing community. Fishers may be connected through alternative community social groups, especially if they have children who participate in community activities. Therefore, to understand the social and community impacts of policy and economic change, we need to develop a better understanding of how fishers "fit" within their residential community, along with the competing interests and dilemmas that may hinder fisheries management. Knowing how fishers are socially tied to their communities will also help us understand the human capital needs of fishers and the ways in which both the community and individual fishers can best enhance their human capital opportunities.

## What Is Meant by "Human Capital"?

Human capital theory, primarily an economic orientation, suggests that human capital (for example, education, job experience, acquired skills) is linked with labor market outcomes.[5] Furthermore, individual decisions to invest in human capital are related to local labor market opportunities. Investment in education by businesses and individuals has been shown to enhance occupational options and performance. However, if jobs are unavailable in the first place, residents who invest in additional education and training risk being overqualified for existing jobs. This suggests that investment of human capital might be a combination of individual motivation and employment opportunity.[6]

Johnson and Stallman suggest that the lack of economic activities available in the community may reinforce an individual's underinvestment in human capital.[7] That is, if individuals perceive that they can obtain a good job without much education, they have little incentive to continue in school. However, if those well-paying or stable jobs are lost or become unavailable, individuals, families, and communities without investments in local human capital are at a disadvantage to develop alternative employment. The downside for local residents is that the lack of a broad range of skills might result in high unemployment should the dominant industry leave, experience a decline, or undergo technological innovations. Furthermore, the idea that many natural resource-dependent communities have previously experienced intermittent periods of economic prosperity (for example, cycles of boom and bust) has unfortunately contributed to a lack of investment in local human capital.[8] This perception might prove especially relevant in fishing-reliant communities because of the seasonal nature of the industry. Focusing on fishing-reliant families and communities provides a needed understanding of the role of human capital in the ability of families and communities to adapt to change.

## Communities and Structural Capital Opportunities

This study focuses on three commercial port communities along the Oregon coast. Because commercial fisheries differ across regions, communities were selected based on relative size (small, medium, large port) and geography (representing the southern, central, and northern coasts). Within each community 15 commercial fishing families and 15 nonfishing families were interviewed, for a total of 30 families in each community. The 90 in-depth interviews were conducted over a six-month period from 1996 to 1997. Although the interview sample was relatively small, the results clearly indicate a trend in which competing community interests disagree about the direction residential places ought to be heading. Respondents reflect a diversity of occupations and lifestyles. There are likely to be cultural differences across fishers based on gear type and fishery, yet they are likely to be connected by their attachment to community; hence the fishers will not be separated in the following discussion.

The three communities selected were Garibaldi (small, northern), Newport (large, central), and Brookings (medium, southern). There are similarities among the three study communities that reflect broader economic trends experienced along most of the coast of Oregon. That is, all of the study communities are experiencing overall economic growth, primarily driven by recreation, tourism, and retirement. Although these communities have turned their attention to tourism as a means of economic sustainability, they typically use their fishing heritage as a marketing tool by promoting fishing events such as the Blessing of the Fleet. As one Newport bay front merchant stated, "People don't come here to buy things, they come to smell the fish."

In general, the merchants interviewed in these communities like the proximity of the commercial fishing industry. Visitors can watch working fishing boats dock, fish being cleaned, and crab pots being emptied. However, the commercial fishers and processors are not as content with the proximity of nonfishing industries. Parking regulations designed to keep traffic circulating mean their employees and customers have to walk or get dropped off while parking elsewhere. Large trucks, essential to the processing businesses, cause an uproar whenever they need to stop in the middle of the narrow, crowded streets. Commercial fishers see tourists being catered to while working fishers have trouble finding dock space and places to unload their fish. The human and structural capital issue of whether or not community-level (and port) interests are meeting the practical needs of the fishers becomes contentious.

The study communities also share drawbacks that have lessened their opportunities for economic diversification. All have transportation, logistical, and traffic problems associated with their natural topography, distance from metropolitan areas, and limited infrastructure. All three communities have common employment problems, namely (1) seasonality of labor and (2) a shortage of workers willing or able to accept relatively low-paying service jobs. Among all of the study communities, there is a general sense that major forces of change (for example, fisheries policy) are beyond their (local) control.

Similar demographic and economic shifts related to the composition of the communities are evident. Not unlike residents of many rural communities, long-time residents and parents are concerned that their children and other young members of the community are forced to leave to find meaningful careers, which is a classic human capital issue—in this case, too much human capital for the available job market. The flight of younger people to larger towns contributes to the communities' becoming increasingly dominated by older citizens. An additional human capital issue that emerges from these three communities is that the workers displaced from declining traditional natural resource industries may not be well suited to jobs that serve recreation and retirement. Moreover, the new jobs created by recreation and retirement often pay less than those lost in traditional industries, such as forestry and fisheries.

When examining human capital within communities, we need to consider the  key factors of community education levels and opportunities. At the high school level, dropout rates for the 1995–1996 academic year range from 4.7 percent in Brookings, to 5 percent in Garibaldi, and 9.4 percent in Newport. All three of the study communities now have regional access to community colleges. Many of the people showing initial interest in attending classes have been retirees in the area, but most areas are starting to see a range of people coming in for educational services. When interviewed, community college administrators indicated relatively little interest among fishers or members of fishing families, however. This may put commercial fishers at a competitive disadvantage should they seek alternative employment as a human capital investment option.

## Linking Fishers to Place

In addition to examining community infrastructure, assessing residents' attitudes toward their community and the role of commercial fishing provides a useful look at the potential issues communities may be facing.

Respondents in this study were initially asked to indicate what they felt were their community's strengths. This question illustrates the amenities that might tie people to a place. Both fishing and nonfishing families in all three communities highlighted their coastal location, relative small size, and moderate climate as strengths of their community. In this opening question, it was evident that although there is a diversity of occupations within these places, there are similarities among residents and their attitudes toward their perceived community strengths.

A second question asked respondents what type of training or career development opportunities they would like to see in their community. Both fishing and nonfishing families in all three communities mentioned computer training and the need to more efficiently use local community colleges. Interestingly, although fishers and their families stress the need to access community college resources, few have taken advantage of available opportunities. Reasons include availability and access to class at times convenient to fishers. Beyond computer training, fishers and nonfishers in all three communities differed on the type of additional training needed in the community. The following two quotations illustrate this difference; the first response indicates a lack of training and jobs, and the second suggests training is available, but there are no jobs:

> When us old guys are gone or retired, who is going to fix the boats and do the fishing? Not many young ones coming in now. They go away, like our son, to find jobs someplace else.
>
> Garibaldi fisher

> The job training is available, WE NEED JOB PLACEMENT.
>
> Newport nonfisher

Another difference between fishers and nonfishers was that fishers frequently mentioned the need for more safety training, crew training, and maritime classes to be held locally whereas nonfishers were less specific. The differing views about the availability of training has important implications for determining future needs and priorities for community development. This lack of agreement poses an interesting issue for local communities (especially as the continued availability of funds for education remains uncertain): when budgets are tight, what types of classes or training should take priority?

An additional set of questions was designed to determine what role commercial fishing has played historically in the development of the community and how important commercial fishing should be for the future

of their community. Response options ranged from 1 (not at all important) to 5 (extremely important). Table 1 illustrates the mean score of
both fishing and nonfishing respondents.

As table 1 illustrates, all respondents from the three communities indicate that historically, commercial fishing has been important to the development of the community. This was not surprising given the settlement
history of these places. However, when respondents were asked about the
role of commercial fishing for the *future* development of the community,
differences emerged. The noticeable trend is the decrease in importance
noted by all respondents. In Garibaldi and Brookings, nonfishing families indicate less future importance than do fishers. However, in Newport,
nonfishers assign a slightly higher level of importance to commercial fishing than do fishers.

The precise explanation for the finding in Newport is uncertain. It
may be the case, as stated above, that nonfishers recognize the importance
of a commercial fishing "backdrop" to other community development
options. Or commercial fishers in Newport might feel a sense of impend-
ing doom for their livelihoods, or possibly a lack of community support
for their industry. An important implication for human capital suggests
that, overall, there may be less support for options that emphasize commercial fishing activities over other community priorities. This hierarchy
of support might lead to conflict over the future directions of financial
and investment opportunities within these communities.

*Table 1. Importance of commercial fishing (means).*

|  | Past | Future |
|---|---|---|
| Garibaldi | | |
| Fishing (n = 15) | 4.66 | 3.38 |
| Nonfishing (15) | 4.67 | 2.90 |
| Newport | | |
| Fishing (15) | 4.39 | 3.00 |
| Nonfishing (15) | 4.39 | 3.27 |
| Brookings | | |
| Fishing (15) | 4.44 | 3.97 |
| Nonfishing (15) | 4.53 | 2.57 |

1 = not at all important
5 = extremely important

A final question asked respondents whether or not their community should maintain the commercial heritage of the area. Respondents in all three of the communities indicated "yes." There was only one nonfisher, from Newport, who said "no." As with the question above on the historical importance of commercial fishing to the community, it was expected that respondents would indicate a positive response. After all, commercial fishing had provided past positive economic and cultural benefits to the community. However, after their "yes" response, a follow-up question of "How?" was posed to each respondent. Answering this follow-up question proved to be more difficult for the respondents, with many people indicating, "I don't know" or "I'm uncertain how, but it should."

When respondents were probed a little more, some interesting responses emerged. One of the themes from fishers centered on the need to educate the public, both locals and visitors, on what exactly commercial fishers do and how they contribute to the economy of the community. As one Brookings fisher put it, "[We] need more positive publicity, don't focus on the negative things."

Other responses from fishers included (1) a need to respect commercial interest, not just the sportfishers; (2) more money poured into bays (for example, dredging), (3) the incorporation of fishing into city planning; (4) the need to support the logistics of fishing (for example, parking); and (5) more community collaboration with fishers.

Nonfishers also had some suggestions for how the community could maintain the commercial fishing heritage of the area. First, the community could work more closely with the fish commission. Second, it could establish and maintain museums/interpretive centers. Third, the community could be "more supportive of fishermen, the new residents don't know or appreciate the port. New residents are wealthy and this means their interests are different than others" (Brookings nonfisher). Finally, the city could maintain the waterfront ("Develop it like a small Monterey, CA"— Brookings nonfisher). The suggestions made by both fishers and nonfishers offer some interesting ideas for human capital development in these (and other) communities, as well as ways to maintain the commercial fishing heritage of the area.

## Conclusions

Residential communities can have a substantial impact on the human capital options of fishers. Although individuals might have different human capital strengths and weaknesses, the residential community might be able to provide a means to strengthen human capital alternatives. Conversely, if the residential community does not embrace the fishing community, the infrastructure support needed for commercial fishing activities might not be given priority.

There is a need to better understand the links between all sectors of the community. Findings suggest that similarities exist among fishers and nonfishers on the importance of commercial fishing to the future of their communities. Although overall support for the commercial fishing ports in these communities was evident, such support by the community may be tenuous, especially given the shifting dynamics (social and economic) associated with shifting economies (for example, resource extraction to tourism and retirement). Many Oregon coastal communities are dealing with the political fallout of shifting tax burdens that affect community amenities (for example, water, sewer, and, in particular, funding for local schools). Therefore, at the local level, competing community interests will severely affect the ability of local ports and management to achieve their fishery goals. Fisheries management cannot ignore such local social systems of interaction and socioeconomic pressure.

Clearly, communities must respond to new and competing demands for public services in meeting basic community needs. This study brings us closer to identifying what the fishing and residential communities have in common (for example, a commercial fishing heritage and educational opportunities) and how future human capital options can be developed that meet the needs of both individuals and the community. The ties to a residential community can bring social support; however, if new regulations or resource constraints force fishers and their families to relocate, the community not only risks a loss of unique human capital skills, but also the cultural identity that draws new residents and visitors.

## Notes

1. T. Bender, 1978, Community and Social Change in America (New Brunswick: Rutgers University Press); W. R. Freudenburg, 1989, Social Scientists' Contribution to Environmental Management, *Journal of Social Issues* 45: 133–152.

2. A. Davis, and C. Bailey, 1996, Common in Custom, Uncommon in Advantage: Common Property, Local Elites, and Alternative Approaches to Fisheries Management, *Society and Natural Resources* 9(3): 251–266.

3. J. Gilden, ed., 1999, *Oregon's Changing Coastal Fishing Communities* (Corvallis, OR: Oregon Sea Grant); G. Munro, N. Bingham, and E. Pikitch, 1998, Individual Transferable Quotas, Community-Based Fisheries Management System, and "Virtual" Communities, *Fisheries* 23(3): 12–15.

4. Davis and Bailey 1996.

5. C. R. Humphrey, G. Berardi, M. S. Carrol, S. Fairfax, L. Fortmann, C. Geisler, T. G. Johnson, J. Kusel, R. G. Lee, S. Macinki, N. L. Peluso, M. D.

Schulman, and P.C. West, 1993, *Persistent Poverty in Rural America (Boulder,* CO: Westview Press)

6. Humphrey et al. 1993.

7. T. G. Johnson and J. I. Stallmann, 1994, Human Capital Investment in Resource Dominated Economies, *Society and Natural Resources* 7: 221–233.

# Families

# CHAPTER 6

# Reconstructing Identities, Families, Communities, and Futures in the Wake of Fisheries Regulation

*Helen J. Mederer and Christopher Barker*

The consequences of industry management for fishers and their families are multiple and interwoven. In a four-year study of commercial fishing families in Point Judith, Rhode Island, we observed several human components to the aftermath of recent regulation. These social consequences of fishery management need to be understood to facilitate effective strategies for promoting positive adaptation within fishing communities. The impacts of regulation are felt in three domains of human existence: the self (identity), family, and community. The renegotiation, indeed the reconstruction, of these domains must be recognized as an integral part of the overall adaptations that fishers and their families are making to their profoundly altered conditions. This paper characterizes these re-negotiations of human experience in Point Judith and offers some of their implications for future decisions and remediation efforts by industry management. The study described in this paper, conducted between 1992 and 1997 with funding from Rhode Island Sea Grant, focuses on the consequences of Amendments 5 and 7 of the New England Fishery Management Council's (NEFMC) Multispecies Ground-

We thank Angela Caporelli of the Rhode Island Seafood Council for numerous enlightening conversations, access to, and insights about the fishing industry, and Rebecca Brewster for invaluable assistance in the preparation of this manuscript.

fish Plan and the means by which families that make their living from commercial fishing adapt to tremendous change.

## Fishery Management in New England in the 1990s

Amendment 5 of the NEFMC's Multispecies Groundfish Plan, passed in 1994, sought to eliminate overfishing of groundfish (flounder, cod, haddock, sole) within five years, by decreasing fishing effort by 10 percent a year, placing restrictions on the mesh size of nets, and enacting several other regulations. Even before these provisions were implemented, fishery scientists realized that they were too little, too late to rebuild groundfish stocks. Thus Amendment 7 was implemented in spring 1996, closing 6,000 square miles of Georges Bank, historically the richest fishing grounds in the Northeast. Net mesh sizes increased again, and quotas were enacted for more species and became more restrictive. The number of days fishers are allowed to fish decreased through days-at-sea regulations. Importantly, an additional measure in Amendment 7 stipulates that new regulations can be implemented on an ongoing basis as new data become available.

## The Study and Sample Characteristics

All of the 23 families in the Point Judith study derived most of their family income from dragging for groundfish. Point Judith is less dependent than most ports in southern New England on traditional groundfish such as cod, haddock, and flounder. In 1991, according to NMFS, only 20 percent of their landings came from these regulated species (in comparison, they made up 85 percent of Gloucester's landings). Point Judith is also unique in that the fishers are less ethnically identified and less dependent on traditional fishing and family practices than fishers in other southern New England ports. An important feature of the Point Judith fishing community is that it is not defined well geographically. Fishers live in many surrounding communities, and there are few neighborhoods that are defined primarily by occupation.

The sample consisted of boat owner-operators as well as deckhands and their wives-partners. All of the respondents were either married or living in a marriagelike relationship. Although the study design aimed at equal representation of both owners and crew, crew were less accessible and less likely to be in long-term relationships. Thus, approximately 80 percent of the sample were boat owners. The respondents have a mean age of 41 years, with females 4 years younger than their husbands, on average. They have an average of 2.4 children, 1.6 living with them. Their average income in 1994 was in the $40,000–$49,000 range, with 53 percent reporting declines in income since 1993. As the study progressed, more than 90 percent of the sample reported subsequent income declines.

## Identities in Flux and Crisis

Identity addresses a basic human need to comprehend and value who we are as individuals and creates a sense of connection to our surroundings and to others. It is created by our interactions with intimate others, work, religion and ritual, and community. Identity influences created meanings, self and other image, affiliation, and commitment. Individual identity also is thought of as a sense of self, whereas collective identity refers to the results of shared experience and makes up the principal binding agent for communities of all kinds.

Fishers traditionally have assigned great importance to their profession in constructing their identities as individuals and as members of society. Fishing requires unique levels of commitment (extended periods of absence from home and community, long hours of demanding labor, and the acceptance of risk), attracts a unique set of character traits and values (independence, solitude, self reliance),[1] and for many has been a matter of family involvement for generations. It is no wonder, therefore, that fishing provides a primary source of meaning in personal experience. Fishing is often described by fishermen and their wives as something that is "in their blood," and they commonly express the conviction that they would be ill-suited for any other occupation. The salience of this occupational identity and the resulting commitment to fishing as a way of life exemplify the tremendous resiliency and adaptability of fishing families. As one wife of a fisherman explained, "Although it's a pain-in-the-neck way of life, it is a way of life that becomes so much involved in your whole life that I think it would be hard just to give it up and walk away."

The passing of Amendments 5 and 7 of NEFMC's Multispecies Groundfish Plan, and the conditions leading up to the legislation, precipitated great upheavals in the identities fishers had forged around their occupation. Characteristics of the industry that fishers value so highly, such as independence, self-determination, solitude, control, and financial reward, were compromised in a short time. Thus was the identity of "fisherman" challenged. The unique conditions and demands of the profession had attracted individuals with those character traits that were demanded, supported, and reinforced by the traditional structure of the industry. Over time, a mutual adaptation had occurred, largely through negotiations of identity based on long-term individual and collective experience.

Fishing is an inherently uncertain occupation: the risks are high and the catch is relatively unpredictable in the short term.[2] In the wake of resource depletion and regulation, however, this uncertainty extends to the ability of fishers and their families to make an adequate living from fishing in the long term. One wife expressed the following sentiment: "I don't like going [to the boat] anymore because it's stressful, because you have this envelope of bills and there's our little paycheck. It's scary, it's like, how much longer can we hang on?" Thus fishers are forced to reevaluate the extent to which they define themselves in terms of their occupation. Their emotional commitment to fishing as a way of life, their customary reluctance to consider alternative sources of income, and even their identity as family provider through fishing are called into question. The following statements capture the essence of the identity transformations affecting fishers as they face highly uncertain futures.

> I started fishing when I was 13. Now I'm 49, and it's something I really love. I fish because I like what I'm doing and I have to keep food on the table, but I can do equally as well at anything. My biggest fear is when I can't fish anymore, what will I be like? What will be the repercussions of my self-worth? Did I make a big mistake? A lot of question marks.

One wife remarked:

> The more restrictions that come, he could be out of business, which will definitely impact us as a family and in terms of who he is as a person. Because he is a fisherman, that's who he is. So it can really be a mess.

## Renegotiating Family Roles and Strategies

Each of the families in our sample employed a unique blend of strategies and role boundaries to cope with the demands of fishing prior to Amendments 5 and 7. Without exception, the changes rendered by Amendment 7 invoked renegotiation of these family strategies.

Traditionally, fishing families relied upon a division of labor based on gender, with husbands in charge of breadwinning and wives in charge of maintaining home and family. Wives, however, were required to orchestrate two distinct adaptations to the fishing way of life. One set of family routines centered around the fishermen's absence and is often described by wives as the more "normal" flow of family life. For instance, one wife explained,

> I don't need somebody else here to make everything all right. . . . One of my first questions when he comes in is, "when are you going fishing again?" because he has come in and invaded my territory. And he will say, "oh, a couple of days," and that's O.K.

The second routine involves accommodating the return of the fisherman into home and family and creating for him some meaningful role in and access to the family. The following excerpts from interviews with two wives of fishermen vividly illustrate these adjustments:

> It's like an interference, an intrusion, you get so used to making your own decisions, coming and going as you please, really being your own boss. . . . It's like leading a dual life. You have to almost flip; you're independent, and then you play a game. . . . When he comes home and says, "Did the kids have supper yet?" it's insulting, and yet you try and understand where they are coming from. They want to feel involved, but imply that when he's not here, the kids don't get dinner. All of a sudden someone is coming in and wants to have some involvement with the family. He is trying in his own way to be involved. So you flip the hat just to pacify them for a few days.

And:

> I like to sit down for dinner. I don't like it when he—and he does this a lot—he'll come in and I'll just be putting dinner on the table and I'll go and get his dish . . . and he'll say, "I'm not hungry." And then nobody wants to sit down because Daddy is home. So that is an intrusion. But I don't think it would be fair to say, "well, look, if you cannot be here for dinner, do not come in and interrupt our dinner." He's only here for one day, and I would feel like a witch if I said that.

Words like "intrusion" and "interruption" were commonly used by wives to describe this life of constant adjustment in roles and duties, in power and decision making, and in family membership. This constant renegotiation of routines and roles becomes normal and predictable. Wives learn to value their independence and see no contradiction between it and their economic dependence upon their periodically present husbands. Families endure this strategy for several reasons: to allow fishers to do and be what they love and to reap the financial rewards of fishing.

Under the regulations imposed by Amendment 7, however, husbands and fathers are home more often, with either no paycheck or a paycheck that reflects a decreased ability to perform their main family role. Men are thus losing their "ticket" to family life and are occupying a space in family interaction that is not normally available to them and in which they have, at best, limited roles. Whereas income derived from fishing has declined for most families, the rhythms and routines of family life continue to revolve around the special demands of fishing—the demands of the boat, of the weather, and of pursuing and selling the catch.

Amendment 7's stipulation that regulations could be changed and imposed as data became available about various species means that families cannot merely "adjust" to one new reality. Fishers no longer have control over when, what, where, and how they fish. This is stressful to families, who already live with unpredictability. The limited planning they could do now is gone, and this frustrates many. The established nature of their lives, the rhythm of the unpredictability, has changed. One wife, whose husband's ability to fish was directly affected by regulations when he was unable to obtain new licensing for a boat that was being repaired, described their family life this way:

> Now that we're together all the time, I'm not used to it . . . and I do need my space. I'm just a person who likes to go in a room and close the door. . . . But now it's like I walk in the door, and he is right there. . . . I liked it when he would go out on three trips and have one home . . . For those two-thirds [of the year when he was gone] I could handle it. I finally found a balance, and now it's *pffft*. Down to how we do the dishwasher. We never had these picayune things before because we didn't have time.

Another wife described what happened after a boat accident coincided with more stringent regulations:

> He was tied up at home all winter—fished off another boat, so he was only gone half the time. And that was a real difficult adjustment. It was funny, because the kids would look at him and say, "that's not how we do things around here, Dad." And it was more difficult for him, because I think it really hit him how much of a life we had built without him.

Of course, tremendous variation exists in the fisher's sense of belonging within the family and the extent to which he is integrated into the family routine. Some fishers, presumably those who identify most strongly with their occupation and exemplify some of the character traits rewarded by fishing (preference for solitude, control, and so on), prefer to maintain rigid gender boundaries between work and family. A startling commentary to that effect follows:

I love fishing. It's a man's world. . . . My whole philosophy of suburbia is, you ought to put a big fence around it, and men ought to come alongside and throw money over the side and go back to where they belong. I really don't fit in here. . . . It's nice being home, it's nice having weekends, it's nice to be able to sit here . . . but I, my brain, always goes back to the boat.

Another husband expressed a more common preference for separation of work and family along gender lines:

We've had 25 years of a successful marriage. . . . My wife has done a wonderful job of raising our children and maintaining our home and our family. It's up to me to earn the money for necessities.

Some wives also prefer separate domains and express resentment at how the regulations are testing their family organization. The following quotations come from wives whose husbands were having a difficult time remaining in fishing:

No, I don't [work outside the home]. I tried it for awhile. I found it very hard. I hated leaving my child at the day care, and when I got a chance to quit, I did. To tell you the truth, I'd rather be poor. I haven't worked in 22 years.

Well, the only issue that bothers me right now is the fishing thing. I told him not to talk to me about it. I have enough to worry about, the kids, the house. He says we are going to starve to death. I don't want to hear that. "You go out and get a job."

Since Amendment 7 went into effect, fishers and their families are finding their customary balance between time at sea and time at home invariably affected. Those who continue to pursue groundfish are limited by the regulations in Amendment 7 and thus are home more often. Those fortunate enough to possess permits for a range of species are able to diversify their target species and increase their effort to compensate for reduced groundfish availability. Whether they are home more or less since Amendment 7 began, the result is the same: an intricate balance of shifting roles and routines achieved over time is thrust into a state of flux and renegotiation. It is where significantly reduced income from fishing has coincided with either increased presence or absence of the fisher within the home that we have observed some of the most trying circumstances for families in transition. That so many families in our sample have been able to endure these cumulative stressors while keeping the family unit intact is one of the greatest testaments to their resiliency.

## Rebuilding Communities

The effects of regulations on individual identities and family organization have led to a third realm of impact—the fishing community. Communities are collectives of people with similar or complementary identities, and so community is the purveyor of collective identity. Community
brings people together through significant networks of social interaction;
shared experience or endurance of hardship; a sense of place and of connection with the past; a sense of belonging and purpose; and a common
set of values, goals, and interests.[3] Recent changes in the fishing industry
continue to exert a destructive influence on the maintenance of community in Point Judith. Given the crucial role that community can play in
directing effective responses to demanding circumstances, and the many
ways it can strengthen families and inform identities, its decline in Point
Judith is a particularly relevant trend in the context of a highly regulated
fishery.

The absence of a neighborhood of fishing families, the absence of any
single predominant ethnic identity or religious affiliation, and the complex set of adaptations to the demands of fishing, forged of individual
identity and family strategies, combine to minimize the community orientation among Point Judith fishers and their families. Of the 23 families
in the sample, 14 described themselves as not being "tied in" to the fishing
community, 5 said that they were "tied in," and 4 reported that they were
somewhat involved in the fishing community. Various reasons were given
for the lack of involvement, such as "we sort of stick to ourselves," and
"we have more in common with the people in our neighborhood." Those
who did report themselves as tied in commented that the small size of the
community enhanced their affiliation with the industry. For instance, one
wife said: "I can't go anywhere or do anything without someone talking
about fishing, you know. Most of his friends are fishermen." Those who
reported some affiliation with the community spoke of how they "knew
everyone" but did not necessarily socialize within the fishing community.

Beginning in the 1970s, the explosive capitalization of the industry
and resultant exploitation of the fisheries resource altered the demograph-
ics and the character of the fishing fleet in Point Judith. Increased variety
in types and scales of fishing operations, varying degrees of economic
success and stability among families, and increased competition among
vessels for a diminishing resource weakened the bonds of collective experience upon which communities depend. The regulations implemented

in response to overfishing further obstructed the maintenance of community in Point Judith.

The applied social sciences, and the organizations and agencies that fund them, have come to view maximum community participation as the primary criterion for successful, self-sustaining, community endeavors. Still, there is an overwhelming sense in Point Judith that many of the decisions that directly affect fishing families are made behind closed doors. This impression has a demoralizing effect on communities. The families in our sample were particularly vocal in expressing a sense of powerlessness in influencing the regulatory process. They invariably agree that some regulation is needed and that overfishing did occur, but they consider many of the requirements wasteful and inconsistent. Public hearings were held before each successive round of regulation was implemented, but fishers sensed that their input was largely ignored. The focus and programs of community organizations, such as the Galilee Fishermen's Resource Center,[4] also suffered from this lack of community involvement in the decision-making process. The difficulty the center encountered in securing financial backing and engaging the support and enthusiasm of the larger fishing community reflects this organizational inadequacy.[5]

And yet, critical elements of a viable community in Point Judith periodically announce their persistence. Until its recent collapse, Point Judith operated a fishermen's cooperative that offered competitive prices for their catch. The closing of the co-op was both cause and consequence of the decline in community. Yet, the adaptive nature of community in responding to crisis was evidenced following an oil spill off the coast of southern Rhode Island during a storm in January 1996. The North Cape oil spill had an immediate and severe impact on both inshore and offshore fishers of all types. Lobstermen and scallopers were particularly hard hit; however, all fisheries were severely affected by the destruction and damage of habitat, cleanup efforts, and closed areas. The community, through the Fishermen's Resource Center, promptly organized a Fishermen's Relief Fund, which disbursed emergency provisions of home heating fuel (ironically enough, it was home heating oil that spilled), food, and money for those families hardest hit by extensive closures of nearshore fishing grounds. The potentially devastating blow that this event predicted was mitigated through community action. Additionally, there remains in southern New England a strong tendency for fishing vessels to take active roles in assisting disabled or missing vessels. The community administers a scholarship fund that is supported by annual community fund raisers and has hosted events such as "old-timers day."

These examples of economic cooperation, collective responses to crisis, sense of mutual commitment, and recognition of collective identity suggest not the absence of community, but rather the persistence of a community whose viability has been challenged and whose salience has been heightened by a common crisis.

A renewed sense of community in Port Judith might lead to greater involvement of the town in determining its own future. However, several issues work against the re-creation of the Point Judith fishing community. One issue that affects community transition and individual identities is the lack of planning for future fishing industry workers. In New England, the ocean is a primary basis for economic activity. Our data indicate that there most likely will be intergenerational attrition in commercial fishing; however, the sons and daughters of commercial fishers still are embedded in the culture of the fishing industry and love the ocean. There is a need, therefore, to provide a link to the marine trades of the future.[6] Charter schools might be developed that build a liberal arts and science curriculum around marine activities. These schools could prepare children for the marine trades, aquaculture, and seafood industries, including boat building, engine repair, and marketing. In addition, such schools might also provide certification training for OSHA programs such as HAZMAT, which covers the handling of hazardous materials.

In Point Judith, neither the regulations themselves nor the remediation efforts directed toward the seafood industry have recognized the uniqueness of this port. Point Judith historically has been relatively innovative. For instance, Point Judith fishers realized 15 years ago that groundfish were being seriously depleted and undertook a major effort to diversify their fishing efforts. They developed new fishing techniques and a market of mackerel, kalamari (squid), and other less popular species and turned their efforts to developing and marketing these newly exploited fisheries. Thus, their reliance on groundfish was lessened. However, when days-at-sea regulations for groundfish came about under Amendment 7, they were based on historical catch data, and Point Judith fishers received fewer days at sea, in effect punishing them for their voluntary endeavors at relaxed effort. In addition, because fisheries are regulated on an area-by-area basis (for example, Georges Bank, the Gulf of Maine), the regulations have an economic impact through displaced effort on areas far beyond the immediate fisheries that are regulated. Thus Point Judith fishers feel first, that regulations did not reward them for creating new markets and new fisheries and, second, that "their" fisheries are being invaded by former groundfishing fishers who are taking advantage of the markets in squid and mackerel. In general, regulators need to reward innovation, look at entire regions, and attend more directly to the economic issues of displaced effort.

Finally, an important issue that fishers feel is misunderstood by federal and state regulators is that of long-term habitat restoration. The problem of fisheries decline is complex, and solutions require time and integration. The relatively short-term goals set by Amendment 7, for instance, will not be achieved merely by regulating the behavior of fishers. Industrial pollution and commercial, recreational, and residential development, especially in wetlands, have had serious implications for the loss of natural habitat. Fishers and the fishing industry have been blamed almost exclusively, and fishery restoration has focused on regulation of the fishing industry. There needs to be more formal recognition of the impacts of industry, development, and pollution on the decline of the fisheries. Various constituencies need to recognize the long-term nature of the task and work together to address ecological, economic, and social causes of the decline of various fisheries. Rather than turning fishers against one another, this strategy might find them working together.

Finally, the fishing community might be strengthened by programs that point to its rich history and contributions. The collaboration of communities in the creation of "living" exhibits of their collective identity is becoming increasingly popular as a means for reflecting, expressing, and learning about the common bonds of experience that tie a community together. The concept stems from the belief that "museums and communities should be related to the whole of life. Living museums are concerned with integrating the family home with other aspects of the community, such as the natural environment, economics, and social relationships."[7] The museum-building process might become an opportunity for reflecting on and expressing individual and family identities and, in so doing, might shape a more comprehensive and conscious evaluation of the effects of recent changes for each individual and family that participates in its creation.

## Conclusion

Amendments 5 and 7 of the Multispecies Groundfish Plan inevitably have caused stress that is requiring much individual, family, and community adaptation. Because of the patchwork nature with which the regulations were adopted in response to new data, as Amendment 7 allows, these regulations lack the benefit of extensive reflection and planning. Thus it is important to assess the human dimensions of these changes. Policymakers need to attend to the impacts on identity, families, and communities in order to make regulations that have the best long-term prospects for the industry. We have presented qualitative data on the impacts of fishing regulations and offered suggestions for both future policy and remediation efforts. Looking toward the next generation of industry workers and ensuring adequate training, recognizing the complexity of the fisheries restoration task by working with other regulatory agencies to get "on the same page," and rewarding innovation that allows the industry to continue within ports are important insights from those involved in the fishing industry.  Attending to these points might help preserve individual identities, families' way of life, and fishing communities. We hope this paper helps to clarify the current status and enlighten future decisions about this unique and valuable industry.

## Notes

1. Madeleine Hall-Arber, 1993. "They" Are the Problem: Assessing Fisheries Management in New England, *Nor'easter: Magazine of the Northeast Sea Grant Programs* 5(2): 16–21.

2. John Poggie and Richard Pollnac, 1988, Danger and Rituals of Avoidance Among New England Fishermen, *Maritime Anthropological Studies* 1: 66–78; M. Estellie Smith, 1988, Fisheries Risk in the Modern Context, *Maritime Anthropological Studies* 1: 29–48.

3. James Kunstler, 1993, *The Geography of Nowhere* (New York: Simon and Schuster).

4. Galilee is the name of the section of Narragansett, Rhode Island, in which Point Judith is located.

5. The Fishermen's Resource Center (part of the Galilee Mission to Fishermen) closed its doors on December 15, 1997 because of lack of funding and community involvement.

6. This and the following insights were provided by Angela Caporelli, a fishery expert from Narragansett, Rhode Island. Ms. Caporelli was the director of the Fishermen's Resource Center and currently is employed by the Rhode Island Seafood Council in South Kingstown, Rhode Island. In this capacity she is spearheading a number of efforts aimed at helping the seafood industry survive. The first author of this paper has found Ms. Caporelli's knowledge and insights about the New England fishing industry invaluable in her research.

7. Nancy Fuller, 1992, The Museum as a Vehicle for Community Empowerment: The Ak-Chin Indian Community Ecomuseum Project, pp. 327–365 in I. Karp et al., eds, *The Politics of Public Culture* (Washington, D.C.: Smithsonian Institution Press).

## CHAPTER 7

# A Multimethod Research Project on Commercial Fishing Families: Multiple Windows on Resilient Women and Families

*Anisa M. Zvonkovic, Lori A. McGraw,*
*and Margaret Manoogian-O'Dell*

## Introduction

This paper provides an overview of a multimethod study focusing on relationships within commercial fishing families. By presenting the varied methods we used to probe the lifestyles created by commercial fishing families, we demonstrate how we come to conclusions about the diversity of fishing marriages. Through an understanding of the rationale, strengths, and limitations of particular methods used in this study, managers will be better able to evaluate data provided to them about families. The combination of methods we used also allows us to draw conclusions about family relationships on a variety of different levels that are useful to policymakers.

Typical scientific methods give us a limited picture of family life. They rely on quantifiable, objective data more suited to an understanding of the economics of fishing than to the relationships within a fishing family. Typically, policymakers and managers are more familiar with these traditional scientific methods than with those used by social scientists. Social scientists often gather information in ways that allow people to talk about their lives. This approach is more valid, since it represents the reality of their lives more accurately than does a strictly economic profile. Social scientists also have to consider such issues as respondents' candor, their errors (based on their subjective perceptions of their lives), and their willingness to discuss their lives. For this reason, social scientists often use more than one method of gathering information so that what they might find using one method can be supported and confirmed with other methods. Social science researchers, and family studies scholars in particular, have developed measures unique to their fields in response to the challenges involved in researching intimate topics.

Managers and policymakers should not be expected to become family studies scholars in order to recognize, and aim to mitigate, the impacts of fishery regulations on families. Still, an understanding of and appreciation for social science research will be helpful to them. To cultivate such an appreciation by demonstrating how distinct methods yield varied results is one goal of this paper. Another, related, goal is to demonstrate the diversity of families, which will be shown as a result of our multiple methods. Families involved in fishing differ from each other in multiple ways and change over time as well. Recognizing diversity in families is critical for policymakers and program managers so that they can design policies that have minimal impact on most fishing families and buffer the impacts of policies on fishers and families who are most vulnerable.

Table 1 shows the various data collection methods we used and presents a brief description of the type of information we gathered with each method. Certain methods are generally understood as better than others at providing reliable and valid data concerning each phenomenon.[1] For example, as shown in the first row and column of table 1, researchers interested in gathering candid feelings and attitudes about deeply personal topics must provide opportunities for individuals to express themselves. It is best if rapport can be established through personal contact with respondents. In this study, we chose to use focus groups of commercial fishing wives in order to understand their attitudes and feelings. The "support group" atmosphere cultivated during the meetings allowed women to disclose feelings they may have denied or downplayed in other settings. To document the behaviors of individuals and families in commercial fishing families and the ways in which these behaviors may change, depending on the husbands' absences while at sea, we needed a more complex method. A relatively new procedure, termed behavioral self-report, was used in this study, as summarized in the second column of table 1.[2] The procedure requires respondents to engage in prearranged telephone interviews in which they report on behaviors they have performed during the previous 24-hour period. One series of interviews was done when husbands were at sea and another was done when they were home. Finally, the last column of table 1 summarizes the survey portion of the project. We used surveys primarily to compare the attitudes and measures of well-being that were normed and standardized on nonfishing populations to a commercial fishing sample.

Gathering data with a variety of methods helps to overcome the drawbacks of each method. It is important to emphasize that a multimethod project will yield more valuable insights, obtained with more reliable methods, than a project using a single method or one relying on individuals' anecdotal reports or common beliefs. Our project used multiple methods. In addition, we paid close attention to change in families. A metaphor we often use to describe the information we gathered comes from photography. By focusing a zoom lens inside commercial fishing families, we were able to look at change in the families over time. We used time-

*Table 1. The multimethod approach to studying commercial fishing families.*

| Focus Groups with Wives | Behavioral Self-Reports with Couples | Survey |
|---|---|---|
| Useful for understanding concerns and learning multiple opinions | Useful for obtaining reports of specific behaviors | Useful for getting measures of well-being that can be compared to nonfishing populations |
| Women participated in group discussions about family lives.<br>• Women's feelings about the fishing family lifestyle<br>• Women's perceptions about family life when husbands are at sea and at home<br>• Women's involvement in the fishing industry and in community activities<br>• Women's perceptions of the context of the fishing industry (e.g., fishery of husband, schedule, government regulations, changes in industry) | Husbands and wives were interviewed separately about behavior during same time period.<br>• Household and parenting tasks and activities<br>• Leisure activities<br>• Couple behavior (e.g., intimate behaviors, conflict)<br>• Fishing business activities<br>• Daily reports of marital satisfaction; happiness; stress; emotional closeness with spouse; power in regard to spouse | Husbands and wives responded to mailed surveys.<br>• Feelings about fishing as a job and the fishing family lifestyle<br>• Background information<br>• Attitudes about marital and work roles<br>• Perceptions of social support in community<br>• Marital and family satisfaction and individual well-being |

elapsed photography, in that we examined the broad sweeps of time that our informants recalled as they characterized changes in their lives. We also compared a time-elapsed picture of family life when the fishers were at sea to when they were home.

## Focus Groups

In the initial phase of our study, we conducted three focus groups made up of wives of commercial fishermen.[3] From this method, we hoped to obtain a general understanding of women's perceptions of their behaviors, as well as their feelings about the fishing family lifestyle. We carried out three focus groups of between three and eight participants at three major Oregon ports. Guiding questions used by the focus group facilitator are listed in the Appendix. It is important to note that the women's answers to each question contained a great deal of information. The discussion had an interactive and spontaneous quality, more like a support group than a formal interview. The focus group meetings lasted two hours each, and each yielded transcripts of over 20 single-spaced pages. The strength of this method lies in the ability of the focus group facilitator to create an open atmosphere in which participants' feelings and ideas can be shared. In this particular method, a camaraderie developed among the women in each group. A pitfall of the method can be that women want to present themselves and their marriages in a positive light. In this study, the facilitator took care to probe for differing viewpoints and to elicit follow-up comments from the women, which can be done more easily in a live interview setting than through written material.

Results of the focus groups demonstrated that women, over time, became increasingly involved in the fishing industry and their involvement reflects their resilience.[4] Initially, many wives regarded the fishing industry as their husbands' work, which took their husbands away from them. Later, they came to view themselves as active members of the fishing community, with an advocacy role to play in the industry. We saw variability, however, in how women regarded their involvement in the industry, depending in part on how long their family had been involved in commercial fishing and on how extensively the women had been formally involved in the industry.

Women and families have been creative in responding to the industry context and its changes. Examples of the advocacy activities of fishing wives were their work on health insurance and safety regulations and their exchange of social and material support with other fishing families. Women voiced concerns about retraining opportunities for their husbands in their communities. Note that these comments, raised at every focus group, emerged from the women's conversations with each other, not from the guiding questions. Through working together on these issues, women gained a sense of solidarity with other fishing families.

## Behavioral Self-Reports

A series of behavioral self-report telephone interviews was scheduled with wives and husbands in the second phase of the study. These interviews were designed to investigate if patterns of family behavior changed, depending on whether the husbands were at sea or home. Five calls were made to wives when husbands were at sea, and five calls were made to wives and husbands when husbands were at home. When husbands were at home, marital partners were called separately, but on the same day, so spouses reported on activities occurring during the same time frame. Interviewers were trained in family studies and communication and employed a computer-assisted telephone interview procedure. The procedure is described in depth in the literature.[5] As with other uses of this procedure, couples were oriented to the project and committed to completing the series of calls. Couples were phoned at scheduled times when they believed they would be home. These aspects of the method meant that the calls were not random and couples could behave differently when they knew they would be called. However, reliability studies of the procedure indicate that couples may act differently for their first call, but the novelty wears off.[6]

In our study, respondents were given sheets that listed the various activities. They could record their activities (household work, fishing business work, leisure activities, as described in the Appendix) before the call and refer to the sheet during the interview. Other variables are listed in table 1. Every question during the call related to the period of time from 5 P.M. the day before the call until 5 P.M. the evening of the call. The procedure required a great deal of dedication on the part of respondents and interviewers. It is worth noting that this procedure can be quite costly, both in terms of the expense of telephone calls and in interviewer and respondent time.

To provide a flavor of the richness of the behavioral self-report data, we present case studies of three different couples. They were selected because they demonstrate some of the range of differences evident in commercial fishing families. In no way is this information a complete picture of the family lives of commercial fishing families, but it does demonstrate key factors that differed among families: fishing schedules, ages of children, and paid work for women and involvement in the fishing business. A final aspect of variability in fishing families is demonstrated by how the marital partners organized their personal lives around themselves, each other, or their children.[7]

### Becky and Tim.

Becky and Tim had school-aged and preschool children, and an infant who was born during the course of the study. They had been married 15 years. Becky had a professional job, and Tim fished for salmon, crab, and other fish. Becky worked 40 hours a week, and she averaged spending just under one hour a day on fishing business activities, regardless of whether she worked or her husband was home. From multiple sources of data, theirs could be characterized as a "couple-centered family."[8] This term means that they oriented their lives to their marriage relationship rather than to their work, other social relationships, or their children. From their daily reports, they were highly satisfied with their marriage. Except for one day, their marital satisfaction scores were either 1 or 2 on a scale of from 1 to 7, with 1 being completely satisfied. When Tim was home, he reported four hours a day engaged in leisure activities with Becky . When he was at sea, she did most of her leisure alone, with activities such as reading. The couple spent quite a bit of time in each other's company and with their children.[9] From Becky's reports, her daily activities were regular and consistent, whether or not Tim was home or at sea, reflecting the "periodic guest" pattern.[10]

### Sue and Bruce

Sue and Bruce had been married for more than 20 years. They had teen and preteen children. Sue had a professional, full-time job, and they owned the boat as well. She was very involved in the business, though her involvement was variable, depending on her paid work schedule. Still, she averaged 90 minutes a day on fishing business activities. This couple, when considered globally, was quite work oriented, to the extent that they could be termed "autonomy centered." This couple's marital satisfaction, from their daily reports, was quite low; Bruce's ranged from 6 to 7 on a scale of from 1 to 7, with 1 being completely satisfied and 7 being completely dissatisfied. This couple's pattern of leisure activities reflected separate lives:

Sue engaged in much more leisure when Bruce was home than when he was at sea. There was one notable exception: one day when he was at home, she was working, she had no leisure activities, and the couple didn't interact at all. Sue and Bruce seemed to have about the same amount of time in leisure activities, which was unusual. For most couples, husbands have more leisure time than wives.[11] Sue and Bruce were much more variable in their daily activities and satisfactions than the other couples. They seemed to devote more of their time to activities with children that often didn't include the marital partner. Their daily lives did not revolve around each other, in that Sue's life was relatively unchanged regardless of whether Bruce was home or at sea. Sue illustrates the independence of commercial fishing wives, which was found in most of the wives in our study.

## Hannah and Joel

Hannah and Joel, a younger couple, had been married eight years and had only very young children. Hannah did not work for pay outside the home, although she did have a college education. Hannah was less involved in fishing business activities than other wives in the study, perhaps because Joel was involved in the fishing business with his father. Hannah engaged in roughly the same amount of leisure activities whether Joel was at sea or not. Theirs could be characterized as a child-centered marriage, in that they spent lots of time with their children, and the wife's day varied little, depending on whether or not the husband was home.[12] He was merely included in their regular activities if he was home.

## Conclusions from the Self-Reports

Taken together, the information about couples' daily activities gathered from behavioral self-reports offers several lessons. Couple diversity is clear. Some couples spend time together in leisure and family work activities when husbands are home, and some do not. Couples vary in terms of how much leisure they have and with whom they spend their time: for example, some husbands have a great deal of leisure when they are home, others do not. Few wives in our study experienced time in leisure that even approached the amount of time husbands experienced when they were not at sea. Different patterns of leisure activity in daily family life would be challenged in different ways by changes in the schedule of fisheries and by moving out of the industry. Increased restrictions on seasons or catch would yield different family impacts, depending on the family's leisure patterns. Such changes are likely to force fishers to fish farther away for longer periods of time, or to leave the industry altogether. For family-centered or child-centered couples, decisions to remain in the industry and spend more time away from home would create additional strain on the family. Yet for families in which husbands have separate leisure lives, such changes may have minimal impact. If fishers opt to leave the industry, the family's pattern of leisure should be considered as they make choices about new occupations. For families in which husbands experience solo leisure (without children or spouse), new occupations that would translate into husbands' being home more often might also create stress for those families. Such families might be encouraged to consider other occupations that involve periodic absence.

## Surveys

In tandem with the behavioral self-reports, we created a survey to measure attitudes and well-being of commercial fishing husbands and wives. The measures on the survey, by and large, had been used to study individuals and families in other contexts.[13] These measures (listed in the Appendix), along with questions concerning the specifics of their fishing family business, were sent to individuals participating in the behavioral self-report portion of the study. Surveys were also sent to a random sample of individuals who held commercial fishing licenses from selected major ports in the Northwest. Both husbands and wives were sent surveys, and the data are analyzed by couple so that differences between the pair can be ascertained. There are 74 completed surveys. Since the measures of job satisfaction and job conditions were developed from a broad cross section of occupations, the data from the surveys allow us to compare commercial fishers' job experiences with those of workers in other occupations. The data also allow us to compare the individual, marital, and family well-being of commercial fishing families with the average levels of well-being of Americans, since the measures used are highly regarded in the field and are standardized.

Preliminary results indicate that the nature of the fishers' jobs is quite different from other occupations on which the measures had been standardized. Fishers spend more time on their job than other workers, averaging 9 months of work a year, 22 days a month, with work responsibilities 24 hours a day. Fishers have little control over their work hours, but a great deal of autonomy at work, when scheduling work activities. These facts about fishers' work conditions would not be surprising to any one involved in the industry. Fishing is such an unusual occupation, however, that the measure of work conditions had elements that did not seem relevant to many respondents, most of whom were boat owners. When fishers and their families, as well as policymakers, consider the future of the industry and the men's occupational futures, the conditions of fishing as a job should be considered. At the same time, the scores of fishermen and their wives on marital satisfaction, family functioning, and psychological well-being are all in the normal ranges, with some variability. Using standardized forms of well-being thus allows us to compare fishing families with other families and to show that they do not differ significantly from a random sample of families on which the scales were normed. Though commercial fishing families experience a highly unusual work context, they are resilient. This fact seems missing from journalistic attention paid to fishing families in crisis. Several respondents actually wrote on their surveys that they were concerned that the information could be used to stigmatize them and portray them as "troubled." We did not find evidence that fishing families experienced greater levels of distress than nonfishing families in other studies using the same measures. It must be acknowledged, however, that the less well-functioning families may not have chosen to participate in the study.

## What Managers and Policymakers Can Gain from This Information

The combination of methods used in this study helps to draw conclusions that result in a number of practical implications for family members, communities, and policy. It is important to realize, however, that drawing attention to diversity among fishing families can downplay the similar challenges they face. In this research project, our results highlighted the diversity that exists, illustrated the creative abilities of fishing families to adapt to their changing contexts, and pointed to policy issues that continue to challenge such families. In this conclusion, we emphasize the implications for managers and policymakers.

### Recognizing Women's Roles in the Industry

Perhaps the most important and most basic implication, first articulated by Abigail Adams when our country was forming, is "Remember the ladies!" Wives of commercial fishing families are a part of the fishing industry. They do productive work for the industry, and they have educated opinions on a variety of industry-related issues. Because their activities and contexts are different from those of fishermen, their viewpoints on many issues are decidedly not the same as their husbands'. They deserve an official voice and place at the table when decisions are being made that affect their lives and their communities.

## Health Insurance and Retraining

Health insurance and retraining were discussed by the women in focus groups, and the lack of opportunities for both was revealed by husbands' and wives' responses to the surveys. Commercial fishing families are underinsured and are aware of their high risk. Currently in the Northwest, a grassroots group of commercial fishing wives is working to solve this problem. Concerning retraining, it is important for decision makers to recognize how fishing differs from other occupations. For individuals considering leaving the industry or training for a supplemental occupation, other occupational options that are similar would be good alternatives to fishing. These would include occupations requiring a good deal of autonomy, initiative, and time commitment. For instance, occupations such as long-haul trucking and entrepreneurial jobs without a lot of interpersonal contact would seem appropriate options. Women discussed how community colleges did not offer opportunities that worked with the fishing schedules of their husbands. Perhaps distance-based educational and vocational opportunities, as well as working in conjunction with existing retraining centers and Cooperative Extension services, would fill this gap.

## Community Development

The community implications of this research suggest that people want to be provided with the opportunities to be involved in the planning of their industry and their communities. Women and families involved in the industry were insistent in viewing their industry as an important component of their community's economy. Communities that are vulnerable to changes in the fishing industry could benefit from a systematic analysis of job alternatives and resources, similar to strategic planning. We suggest that community members who plan community activities need to be informed of fishery management and regulatory decisions and be involved in them. This process already occurs at some levels, but including community college staff, employers, and fishing wives and husbands is important.

Some years ago, there was a movement among policymakers toward developing "family impact statements" that would accompany bills or policy changes.[14] While our survey results lead us to be skeptical of a model that would place commercial fishing families at risk for problems, we do strongly support the notion of articulating family impacts for policy changes relating to commercial fishing. We believe commercial fishing families have important perspectives on policies. Our data have shown that it would be simplistic to conceive of a unitary family impact for a suggested policy change. Rather, anticipated policy changes will affect families in different ways, depending on their internal dynamics, in addition to financial variables and other factors that are more commonly studied. The behavioral self-report method demonstrated diversity in women's involvement in the industry and variation in terms of whether couples were "family centered," "couple centered," or "autonomy centered." These distinctions are useful for understanding how a change involving more or less absence from home on the part of the fisher would affect families in different ways. A next logical step would be to delineate, in a systematic manner, the factors that would be key to understanding how families, in all their complexity, might be affected by industry and policy changes.

## Notes

1. Linda Thompson and Alexis Walker, 1982, The Dyad as the Unit of Analysis: Conceptual and Methodological Issues, *Journal of Marriage and the Family* 44: 889–900; Ted L. Huston and E. Robins, 1982, Conceptual and Methodological Issues in Studying Close Relationships, *Journal of Marriage and the Family* 44: 901–925.

2. Ted L. Huston, 1996, *Designing and Carrying Out a Longitudinal Study of Relationships: Lessons from Pair Project* (Austin, TX: University of Texas at Austin, Department of Human Ecology).

3. Richard Kreuger, 1996, *Focus Groups in Qualitative Research* (Newbury Park, CA: Sage).

4. Helen J. Mederer, 1993, Fishing Space and Family Space: Negotiating Gendered Role Boundaries under Fishery Changes, paper presented at the annual meeting of the Rural Sociological Society, Orlando, FL, August 7–10.

5. Huston 1996; Anisa Zvonkovic and Susan Moon, 1996. *Wives' Perspectives on Their Involvement in Commercial Fishing as a Family Business: Constructing a Fishing Family* (Brookline, MA: Family Firm Institute).

6. Huston 1996.

7. Stephen R. Marks, 1986, *Three Corners* (Lexington, MA: Lexington).

8. Marks 1986.

9. Marks 1986.

10. Mederer 1993.

11. Huston 1996.

12. Marks 1986.

13. Richard H. Moos and Paul N. Insel, 1974, *Work Environment Scale* (Palo Alto, CA: Consulting Psychologists Press); Richard H. Moos, 1974, *Family Environment Scale* (Palo Alto, CA: Consulting Psychologists Press); Linda Beth Tiedje, 1990, Women with Multiple Roles: Role-Compatibility Perceptions, Satisfac-

tion, and Mental Health, *Journal of Marriage and the Family* 52: 63–72; N. C. Morse, 1953, *Satisfaction in the White-Collar Business* (Ann Arbor, MI: Institute for Social Research); M. T. Schaefer and D. H. Olson, 1981, Assessing Intimacy: The Pair Inventory, *Journal of Marital and Family Therapy* 7: 47–60; Robert Norton, 1983, Measuring Marital Quality: A Critical Look at the Dependent Variable, *Journal of Marriage and the Family* 45: 141–151; Anisa M. Zvonkovic and Stephen R. Marks, 1990, Coworker Intimacy in a Small Workplace: A Feminist Inquiry, paper presented at the Annual meeting of the National Council on Family Relations, Seattle, WA., November, 1990.

14. Catherine Chilman, 1991, Working Poor Families: Trends, Causes, Effects, and Suggested Policies, *Family Relations* 40: 191–198.

15. Moos and Insel 1974; Moos 1974; Tiedje 1990; Morse 1953; Schaefer and Olson 1981; Norton 1983; and Zvonkovic and Marks 1990.

16. Mederer 1993.

17. Chilman 1991.

# Appendix:
# Selected Measures Used in Each Method

## Focus Group Guiding Questions[15]

1. What are some of the things you enjoy about being in a fishing family?
2. What are some of your worries or concerns?
3. What kinds of supports have been helpful to you as a fishing family?
4. How, if at all, have your feelings about the fishing family lifestyle changed since you've become a parent?
5. How do you think your family changes when your husband is at sea or home?
6. What advice would you give someone who was about to marry someone who fishes?

## Behavioral Self-Report Questions[16]

From 5 P.M. yesterday to 5 P.M. today, which of the following activities did you do? When an activity is done, we need to know with whom you did it, how long it took, and how satisfied you were doing it, on a scale from I–7.

Household tasks (respondents had a list of 21 tasks)
Child care and supervision (from a list of 9 tasks)
Fishing business activities (from a list of 8 activities)
Leisure activities (from a list of 44 activities)

## Survey Measures[17]

Work Factors: Work Environment Scale, autonomy, control
Family Factors: Family Environment Scale, cohesion, control
Work/Family Interaction: Concurrent Role Perceptions Scale
Worker Well-Being: Intrinsic Job Satisfaction Scale
Family Well-Being: Family Environment Scale, satisfaction
Marital Well-Being: Marital Emotional Intimacy
                    Marital Satisfaction
Individual Well-Being: Role Balance Scale
Psychosomatic Symptoms

## CHAPTER 8

# Building Effective Outreach to Fishing Families

*Flaxen D. L. Conway*

## Context

The fishing industry in the Pacific Northwest is a constant challenge. It's a challenge to managers and others responsible for overseeing the industry and to fishers and their families constantly adjusting to changes in the industry. Because of the number of species harvested by myriad vessel and gear types and the complex regulations by species regarding harvest levels, gear types, seasons, and locations and the number of fishers involved, it is nearly impossible for anyone to stay on top of it all.

It's no secret that fishers and fishing families have a well-earned reputation for being fiercely independent. There are several reasons for this. The technical and environmental challenges of commercial fishing require that fishers work alone or in small groups for long periods in a variety of sea and weather conditions. Successful fishers work with little or no direction and make rapid decisions without deliberation or consultation with others.[1] Meanwhile at home, the wife or at-home partner in the fishing business works independently as well, keeping the family together, managing the business and family finances, providing emotional support, and often doing boat or fish sales errands.[2]

Fishing families are known for having strong family ties that help them manage the daily strains of fishing.[3] In fishing communities, women, as well as men, play active roles in establishing and maintaining occupational or community-of-interest relationships. This is because fishers and their families often are isolated from the wider society by the physical location of the work. They restrict leisure time and socializing to work or industry mates and often harbor a sense of belonging that generates an "us against them" social attitude.[4]

Economic change, environmental change, and changes in biological, social, management, and political systems are nothing new to the commercial fishing industry and the families that are its backbone. Resilience, innovation, and endurance have been key coping and adapting mechanisms for these families, their businesses, and the industry. But as these changes began to overlap, the stressors became too great, some of the old coping mechanisms failed to work (buying bigger boats or more gear, fishing longer, and so on), and the family system began to fall apart along with the economy and environment. Interestingly, the same fiercely independent people who choose to live, love, raise children, and earn their livelihoods away from the eight-to-five world that most of us live in are coming to realize that it is at times fundamentally crucial to reach out and work together.

## Our Approach for Reaching Out

The OSU Fishing Families Project (FFP) is an experimental effort—a practical attempt at empowering fishing businesses and families to manage change and maneuver the subsequent transition in a way that provides the most business security and family stability. There are three key components to our approach: peer connectors, skill-building education, and network support.

### Peer Connectors

Our experience with the FFP has taught us that the best way to communicate with fishing families is through peer connectors. Fishers and fishing families tend to trust and learn from each other. In a survey we conducted asking fishers and their families about where and how they obtain information and what their most trusted resources are, their responses indicated that they trust the fishing community first and foremost: "regarding industry issues, over 76% said their most trusted resources were industry sources and co-workers. This was similar for safety issues and seafood issues. For family issues, over 56% said their most trusted resources were co-workers, industry sources, and friends and family."[5]

It's no surprise then that critical to our project were the fishing family coordinators, the fishing family members whom we hired to help us do our outreach into this community of interest over several communities of place. These coordinators were facing the same challenges as all other fishing families these days. And, like the people we were studying, they lived in coastal communities, experienced isolation, coped with separation while their husbands were at sea, struggled through the gear wars, and built skills to share and some connections locally and throughout the community of interest (that is, the commercial fishing family business community).

There were three fishing family coordinators, with regions that covered over 13 small, rural ports or communities along the coastline from southwest Washington to northern California. Some ports have fishing family businesses where the fisher fishes locally and comes home daily. However, in another survey we conducted of the West Coast fishing community, over 62 percent fished out of distant ports.[6] Similarly, in many ports, most of the fishing family businesses engage in several fisheries over the course of the year, depending on the fisheries for which they have permits, market conditions, fishing seasons, and resource availability.[7]

Each fishing vessel is a small business; most are independently owned and operated. In addition, even crew members are considered self-employed by the Internal Revenue Service and work as independent contractors. Fishing families, therefore, are characterized as small business owners, and many family members are involved in the family business—from operating or working on the boat to keeping the books, ordering supplies, and arranging for markets.

The fishing family coordinators provide the critical link to this unique and independent community by supplying personalized contact between the FFP and fishing families. Coordinators work with the project as independent contractors. Their expenses are covered and they receive a modest salary for working roughly .33 to .50 time. They work autonomously and yet are connected and supported by being part of the project team. They are the heart of the FFP.

## Skills-Building Educational Programs and Materials

The FFP delivers community-based tools and strategies for coping with change in a cyclical industry, now and in the future. We help fishing families learn new skills in tracking expenses, managing family and business finances, coping with loss, communicating more effectively, managing during times of transition, and working together more effectively. Listed below is a brief, annotated bibliography of some the publications we have developed as a response to the need expressed by this audience.

### Fishing Family and Business Resource Kit

This resource kit is a compilation of more than 30 brief, practical publications related to managing business and family finances, keeping families strong, and staying in or changing occupations. It also includes a list of local resources for businesses and families.

### Helping Persons Cope with Change, Crisis, and Loss

This educational resource is often requested and used in several regions along the coast by families who lose a member at sea or have faced some other major change in their lives.

### Getting Unhooked from Anger and Conflict

This compilation of practical knowledge grew out of a similarly titled workshop. Even though most people don't feel comfortable talking about conflict, this publication has been one of the most requested in the project. It has been described as helpful both at home with family members and at sea with co-workers.

### Tax Information for Crewmen on Commercial Fishing Boats

This brief, to-the-point publication addresses one of the most critical financial problems in the commercial fishing industry. It was spawned out of the "Staying Afloat/Getting Ahead" workshop.

### Family and Business Records Checklist for Fishing Families

A thorough, practical checklist has been sorely needed for families in the commercial fishing industry. *Family and Business Records Checklist for Fishing Families* was created as a result of the "Staying Afloat/Getting Ahead" workshop.

### Groups That Work

Fishing families are some of the most strongly independent people in the country. And yet the reality is that at times all of us need to work together to support each other. This publication was spawned out of the "Fishing Families Networking" workshops. It contains clear, practical information about forming or reigniting groups, designing group membership, and running effective meetings.

### Letters to Fishing Families

This series of 12 letters is by a writer who was also a fisherman's wife. Created as a practical and educational look at the challenges and rewards of life in a commercial fishing family, each letter deals with pertinent topics, such as keeping in touch, making decisions together and separately, learning when and how to argue fairly, and coping with retirement. The letters prove an excellent educational and validating series for fishing families and for others who want to gain a better understanding of these families and the challenges they face.

### Seeking Professional Help with Emotional Stress and Strain

Many times people can work through problems themselves or with the support of family and friends. Sometimes they need outside assistance from a trained professional. It helps to know where to go for help and who are the people or organizations that could lend some additional support during times of transition.

### Fishing Family Expense Tracking System

Created with the help of several fishing families, this practical, succinct, record-keeping tool can be used as is or customized to fit a fisher's family or business.

In addition to the above publications, the FFP has offered workshops, hosted marine fisheries resource fairs, and created innovative delivery mechanisms (such as teleworkshops or Web-based conferences) in an effort to bring together industry, agency, and political players in a discussion of some of the most current, critical issues facing fishing families and businesses today.

## Network Support

Our experience with the FFP has revealed that the most important resource for individual fishing families and businesses is community-of-interest networks (such as commodity groups and fishermen's wives organizations). We help to assess the existing networks *within* the industry (between fishing businesses or families) and *between* the industry and community and business agencies. We help create or strengthen networks through delivering skill-building opportunities related to communication, leadership, and group process. Learning how to work well together and developing skills such as healthy communication and dialogue, conflict management, and inclusive decision making bring intrinsic rewards to individuals, families, businesses, and the entire community of interest.[8] In this vein, we help to regularly connect over 3,000 fishing families, businesses, and organizations through quarterly, regional newsletters designed and developed by the fishing family coordinators and the local communities.

## How This Network Support Helps Families, the Industry, and Management

The link between management agencies and the industry has been problematic. Fisheries management has traditionally been top down, science based, and bureaucratic—the government decides and acts unilaterally, and fishers are asked to comply.[9] Co-management—the systematic, formal, organized collaboration between the industry and government agencies in the design, implementation, and enforcement of management functions—has been a step toward ending this top-down approach.[10] However, this attempt to forge a two-way process of communication between government and industry is still problematic. One reason is the inability, at this time, of the industry representative on management councils and advisory groups to speak with one voice for the entire industry. Another reason may be that this connection has traditionally been limited to a few industry leaders.

The effectiveness of fishers as participants in the fisheries management process depends on the extent to which they are organized at national, regional, and local levels.[11] Such organization has proven to be problematic for several reasons. There is an incongruity between the fishers' autonomy when fishing and their sublimation of self onshore to cooperative endeavors and organizational goals and needs. This might be why small-boat fishing cooperatives have generally proven unsuccessful. Nevertheless, commercial fishers see the need to participate in the scientific management process to share input and control of decisions affecting their livelihoods.[12]

Consistently and conspicuously absent from representation in fisheries management are the families and communities of people involved in either fish harvesting or fish processing. This is true even though the role of women and the importance of their skills and labor to sustaining fishing enterprises have been documented in the literature.[13] Fishermen's wives often provide crucial organizational, economic, and emotional support for an industry that is otherwise dominated by males.[14] Women constitute a dynamic force in shaping and maintaining a sense of personal identity and group image within the fishing family business community.[15] The work of women in the family business underscores the day-to-day social and economic capacity of men to go fishing.[16]

Recently in the Pacific Northwest, FFP-sponsored workshops have been instrumental in teaching women and families leadership and other skills that help them play more active roles in fisheries management. The FFP-sponsored "Fishing Families Networking" workshops and the *Groups That Work* publication have been directly linked to the creation or strengthening of local fishermen's wives groups. However, even though most of these fishermen's wives organizations managed to overcome the tension, conflicts, and divisiveness often found between commodity groups, they tended to be limited primarily to their community of place. That is until April 1996 when the FFP helped to launch the creation of a regionwide, multigear, multifisheries network called the Women's Coalition for Pacific Fisheries (WCPF).

WCPF's mission is to promote and support a strong local, regional, national, and global fishing industry that connects fishing families and communities in a positive way. With membership that reaches from Alaska to southern California, this community-of-interest network is beginning to extend education and information—that reaches people at the family level—to regional communities of place.

The skills and incentive expressed in WCPF are flowing into other coed groups. One example of this is the West Coast Fishermen's Alliance (WCFA). WCFA is a group of 60 commercial fishing family businesses from Oregon, Washington, and northern California. WCFA is "politically involved and dedicated to preserving the social and economic stability of coastal communities." It was formed in 1994 with the primary focus of opposing the individual transferable, quota management plan for the West Coast fixed-gear sablefish fishery, but it has expanded to reflect its diverse membership (fishing family businesses involved in the crab, tuna, halibut, and rockfish fisheries) and acts as a "voice for small boat fishers from coastal communities all over the West Coast." Their meetings and their network have become more productive and "somewhat orderly, considering the boisterous and opinionated membership," because of leadership and group process training completed by some members who have been involved in FFP programs.[17]

Community-of-interest networks like the two mentioned above could play a key role in helping to inform and educate families, businesses, and the industry about the fisheries management process—the mechanics *and* the importance of their participation. This movement toward cooperation and away from competition is imperative within the industry, between the industry and the Coast Guard, and between the industry and fisheries management.

# Summary

The fishing industry in the Pacific Northwest faces constant challenges. The OSU Fishing Families Project was a practical attempt at empowering fishing businesses and families to manage change and maneuver the subsequent transition in a way that provides the most business security and family stability. We did this through reaching out through peer connectors, delivering practical, community-driven educational programs and materials, and supporting networks.

We believe this approach has been beneficial for individual fishers, fishing families, and the industry. But we also believe it is beneficial for fisheries management because it is helping to increase the effectiveness of fishing families as participants in the fisheries management process. It may not feel comfortable or familiar to anyone involved, but it is a step in the right direction.

# Notes

1. J. S. Thomas, G. D. Johnson, and C. Riordan, 1995, Independence and Collective Action: Reconsidering Union Activity among Commercial Fishermen in Mississippi, *Human Organization* 54(2): 143–151.

2. Dona Davis, 1986, Occupational Community and Fishermen's Wives in a Newfoundland Fishing Village, *Anthropology Quarterly* 59(3): 129–142; Sheila Shafer, 1996, Making Decisions by Consensus: Equal Partners in Power, *Letters to Fishing Families* (Corvallis, OR: Oregon Sea Grant); Suzanna Smith, 1995, Social Implications of Changes in Fisheries Regulations for Commercial Fishing Families, *Fisheries* 20(7): 24–26; V. Thiessen, A. Davis, and S. Jentoft, 1992, The Veiled Crew: An Exploratory Study of Wives' Reported and Desired Contributions to Coastal Fisheries Enterprises in Northern Norway and Nova Scotia, *Human Organizations* 51(4): 342–351.

3. S. Smith and M. Jepson, 1993, Big Fish, Little Fish: Politics and Power in the Regulation of Florida's Marine Resources, *Social Problems* 40(1): 39–49.

4. Davis 1986.

5. 1998 Commercial Fishing Industry Communication Tool Survey, conducted by the OSU Fishing Families Project, funded by Oregon Sea Grant.

6. 1998 West Coast Fishing Community Health Plan Survey, conducted by the OSU Fishing Families Project, funded by Oregon Sea Grant.

7. Jennifer Gilden, ed., 1999, *Oregon's Changing Coatal Fishing Communities* (Corvallis, OR: Oregon Sea Grant); Ginny Goblirsch, Extension Sea Grant agent, personal communication.

8. C. Shaffer and K. Anundsen, 1993, *Creating Community Anywhere: Finding Support and Connection in a Fragmented World* (New York, NY: Tarcher/Perigee).

9. B. McCay and S. Jentoft, 1996, From the Bottom Up: Participatory Issues in Fisheries Management, *Society and Natural Resources* 9: 237–250.

10. S. Jentoft and H. Sandersen, 1996, Cooperatives in Fisheries Management: The Case of St. Vincent and the Grenadines, *Society and Natural Resources* 9: 295–305.

11. McCay and Jentoft 1996.

12. Smith and Jepson 1993.

13. A. Davis and C. Bailey, 1996, Common in Custom, Uncommon in Advantage: Common Property, Local Elites, and Alternative Approaches to Fisheries Management, *Society and Natural Resources* 9: 251–265.

14. R. Dixon, R. Lowery, J. Sabella, and M. Hepburn, 1984, Fishermen's Wives: A Case Study of a Middle Atlantic Coastal Fishing Community, *Sex Roles* 10(1/2): 33–52.

15. Davis 1986.

16. Thiessen, Davis, and Jentoft 1992.

17. John Warner, 1997, *West Coast Fishermen's Alliance: A Short Description* (Charleston, OR: West Coast Fishermen's Alliance).

# Part 2

## Management Challenges

# Loss and Compensation

## CHAPTER 9

## Courses to the 1994 Pacific Northwest
## Coho Salmon Closure

*Courtland L. Smith, Joseph Cone,*
*Jennifer Gilden, Brent S. Steel*

## Background

The Pacific Fishery Management Council implemented a coastwide closure of commercial and recreational fishing for coho salmon in April 1994. Closure of a fishery is an extreme action that is difficult for fishery managers to take. Managers had moved closer to closure in the years before 1994, and continued decline in stock levels left them with no alternative but closure. Although the closure received considerable media coverage in 1994, it resulted from the convergence of many actions over many years.

All coastal fishing communities in Oregon and Washington were affected by the coho closure. These communities are typically small; the largest, Aberdeen, Washington, had a 1990 population of 17,000. Oregon and Washington coastal counties have a total population of less than one-tenth of the states' total. Coho are the major recreational and commercial species for those fishing in the ocean and coastal streams of Oregon and Washington. Salmon fishers include recreationalists who fish in the ocean from private boats and ocean charters, Native Americans trolling in the ocean and netting in the rivers, non-Indian commercial trollers and gillnetters, and anglers fishing from jetties and in rivers. People come to the coast to fish for salmon from the more urbanized Seattle-Tacoma, Portland-Vancouver, and Willamette Valley areas.

The courses contributing to the decline in coho salmon populations include

1. overreliance on hatcheries
2. poor ocean productivity
3. inaccurate scientific assessments of stock abundance
4. excessive fishing pressure
5. detrimental forest, farm, and urban land use practices
6. changing scientific and public attitudes giving greater value to wild and naturally spawning coho

## Converging Constraints on Coho

Since the 1860s salmon management has focused primarily on the number of fish produced and caught.[1] As stocks continued to decline, management restraints increased and became more area- and stock-specific. Seasons became shorter, gears were increasingly restricted, and fishing areas were more confined.

Since the passage of the Magnuson Fishery Conservation and Management Act of 1976, the Pacific Fishery Management Council (PFMC) has had primary responsibility for regional salmon management. The PFMC manages coho and chinook salmon runs from the Mexican to the Canadian borders. Planning for salmon management began under emergency provisions of the Fishery Conservation and Management Act with the 1977 fishing season. The first four of eight management goals were

1. To maintain optimum spawning stock escapement
2. To reduce fishery-caused mortality in nontarget fish (to prevent mortality from hooking and releasing troll-caught salmon)
3. To move toward fulfilling Indian treaty obligations
4. To provide all ocean and "inside" fisheries the continuing opportunity to harvest salmon[2]

The coho closure shows these goals were not met during the 20 years of PFMC management. The causes of coho salmon decline—hatcheries, ocean conditions, inaccurate scientific knowledge, fishing pressure, land use, and social values—are complex and have unfolded over many years.

### Hatcheries

Through the early 1970s, salmon catches grew with increased hatchery production.[3] Hatchery production grew with better feeds, improved disease control, and a shift to releasing smolts rather than fry. Then in the late 1970s and early 1980s, as hatcheries released more coho, production began to decrease. The growth in production proved unsustainable. Studies pointed to problems caused by reliance on hatcheries, and scientists debated their effectiveness.[4]

One problem is that hatchery stocks can sustain higher harvest rates than naturally spawning salmon. Hatcheries increase survival rates for the early part of the life cycle, so a higher percentage of salmon eggs become fry and smolts than they would in the wild. With hatchery fish present, fishery managers set the harvest rates too high, without taking into account the effect of harvest rates on naturally spawning stocks. For the period 1970–83, the estimated fishery impact rate on coho was 80 percent of the natural coho facing mortality from harvest effort (figure 1).[5] Halfway through this period in 1976, ocean survival changed dramatically. Subsequent studies showed that it declined by a factor of five.[6] Naturally spawning runs could not sustain 80 percent exploitation rates, coupled with lower ocean survival.

Another problem is that hatchery management programs were evaluated mainly on the economic efficiency of production rather than on how well they protected biological diversity. Because of this, hatchery fish did not develop the survival traits common to naturally spawning salmon.[7] In addition, economic efficiency goals led hatchery managers to select for

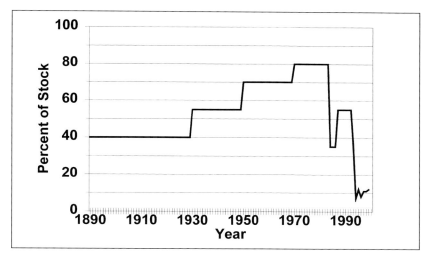

*Figure 1. Estimated coho hatchery harvest rates. Data source: Pacific Fishery Management Council (PFMC), 1997,* Draft Amendment 13 to the Pacific Coast Salmon Plan *(Portland, OR: Pacific Fishery Management Council), 17.*

stocks that were easiest and cheapest to obtain. Hatcheries took fish at the peak of their run, when more are available and collection is faster and less expensive. This practice, combined with the selection of only certain stocks, resulted in less genetic variability.[8] One of the adaptive strategies of salmon is to stray to new habitats, leading to mixing of hatchery and naturally spawning stocks. The lower genetic diversity of hatchery fish reduced the diversity of naturally spawning stocks when the two populations mixed. Hatchery-released fish stray into adjacent watersheds, further influencing genetic diversity. Many fear that diseased hatchery stocks will infect naturally spawning populations when the stocks mix.[9]

## Ocean Conditions

Between 1976 and 1977, a natural shift in North Pacific climatic conditions was correlated with a decline in ocean survival of both hatchery and wild coho. A severe 1982–83 El Niño showed the impact that short-term ocean conditions could have on the growth and survival of salmon, both on juveniles just entering the ocean and on maturing fish.[10] Ocean mortality increases during strong El Niño conditions, and the pre-1976 relationship between upwelling and survival of salmon became progressively less accurate during the 1980s and 1990s. It took more than a decade before these findings became part of management considerations. Poor ocean conditions resulting from this climatic change persisted into the mid 1990s.[11]

In the 1970s, the marine mammal population was very low and the quantity of salmon available for harvest was much larger. By the early 1990s, the reverse was true. Palmisano and others estimate that marine mammals could account for as much as 16 percent of the total take of salmon, while Park claims that marine mammals and birds may take more salmon by weight than are caught by fishers.[12]

Recognition of the impact of ocean conditions challenged the production orientation that had been applied to salmon fisheries. Merely increasing the number of smolts released by hatcheries could not compensate for ocean variability.

## Scientific Understanding

Current understanding of ocean conditions demonstrates that scientific knowledge either lagged behind or was not incorporated into effective salmon management. Significant biases that affected estimates of total salmon numbers were part of the problem. For example, annual stream surveys counted the salmon returning to spawn. Surveys were conducted at a number of sampling sites, and the number of fish was multiplied by stream miles to get a total estimate. The sites where counts were made turned out not to be representative of the salmon production capacities of all coastal streams but instead were selected as "reference sites" where spawning was often concentrated.[13] It was common knowledge among fish samplers, for example, that the sites selected for sampling were often dictated by convenience—proximity to a road or bridge—rather than by some strictly scientific sampling method. These errors continued without adequate scientific review for nearly 40 years.

Another major problem was improperly estimating the stock-recruitment curve. The curve was based on the good years of ocean survival and the incorrect estimate of escapement needs. This led to setting harvest rates too high and decimating wild coho populations. Critics of fishery management argued that these management errors, which favored harvest, showed the institutional bias of management agencies toward their principal clientele, the fishers. Even if the scientific errors were unintended, the bias toward harvest seemed clear enough.

The stock-recruitment model applied to salmon promised maximum sustainable catches—maximum sustainable yield. The model is based on the idea of density dependence, which means that increased survival rates can be achieved by reducing crowding among spawners. The pressure for greater harvest led fishery management agencies to continually set harvest rates that did not recognize the ecological value of salmon carcasses, to not consider the importance of genetic diversity, and to miss the already too-low spawner escapement goals.

Finally, the application of the best scientific knowledge requires resources. The public demanded more services from government during the 1980s and 1990s, and yet legislatures cut funding to agencies and demanded that they be more cost-effective. Fishery agencies had to justify themselves as the population of recreational fishers declined and commercial fisheries became less profitable.[14]

## Fishing

Before 1994, coho were the mainstay of the ocean Washington and Oregon recreational fishery. Because they frequent shallower waters and areas close to shore, smaller recreational boats can easily access them, and charter boat trips for coho could be shorter.

Treaty and nontreaty Indian, commercial, and recreational fishers were allowed to harvest coho at rates of 70–80 percent of the ocean production from 1950 to 1983 (figure 1).[15] These rates led to some of the best coho catches ever. The ocean commercial coho catch off Washington, Oregon, and California in 1976 was 3.8 million fish, and the recreational fishery took 1.5 million (figure 2). By 1993 recreational coho catches were 184,500 and commercial were 77,000.[16] By 1994 the allowable catch of coho was zero.

In 1976 about 2,300 Oregon trollers landed 48 percent of the coho caught in the ocean off Washington, Oregon, and California. In 1994, the number of Oregon trollers landing salmon was 371.[17] The objective of the coho closure was to reduce mortality from fishing. Mortality of coho by incidental catch, primarily in efforts to catch chinook salmon, was cut to 13 percent in the last half of the 1990s.[18] After 1994, management worked to minimize coho bycatch. A very small additional coho mortality occurred after 1994 in a recreational hook-and-release fishery for coho.[19]

Coho catches also were important in the Columbia River. Because of hatchery production, gillnetters increased catches after the mid-1960s. In 1966, lower Columbia coho poundage exceeded chinook for the first time. Since coho are half the size of chinook, this increase represents a very large number of fish. Coho catches reached nearly one million fish in 1986.[20]

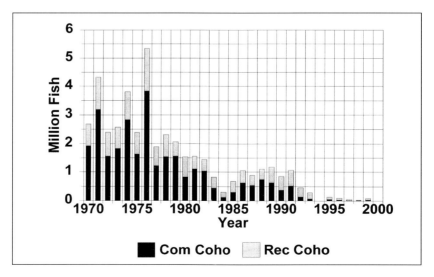

*Figure 2. Ocean commercial and recreational coho catches  Pacific Fishery Management Council, 2000,* Review of 1999 Ocean Salmon Fisheries *(Portland, OR: Pacific Fishery Management Council).*

Most of the coho came from lower Columbia River Mitchell Act hatcheries. Ocean fishing and endangered species problems resulted in limits on coho catch by Columbia gillnetters. Between 1992 and 1994, Columbia River gillnetters averaged less than 53,000 coho each year.

The number of Oregon and Washington commercial gill-net licenses peaked in 1979 at 1,524. They declined to 747 by 1995, partly because of limited entry programs and lack of fishing time. A salmon license buyout program in Washington also helped reduce the number of licenses.[21]

## Land Use

In addition to overfishing, salmon habitat changed by economic activities important to humans without regard to their impacts on salmon.[22] The forest, farm, and urbanization changes most affecting salmon occurred in the 1960s, 1970s, and 1980s. From after World War II through the early 1980s, logging was one of the most significant contributors to coastal economies. In general, before 1987, timber was the largest sector in coastal economies.[23] Logging roads contribute silt that degrades spawning habitat, and poorly designed culverts prevent upstream salmon passage. Logging can also lead to loss of forest cover and woody debris. These losses cause stream temperatures to rise to unhealthy levels and remove protective areas for young salmon.

Agriculture, too, is detrimental because it removes the meanders from streams where coho overwinter; adds pesticides and animal pollution; removes stream vegetation, thus raising water temperatures to detrimental levels; and degrades riparian habitats. In addition, irrigation water is taken from streams during the low-flow summer months. And because many irrigation removals are unscreened, juvenile salmon are taken with irrigation water.

Urbanization has many of the same effects as agriculture. The coastal region of Washington, Oregon, and northern California is not very urbanized, but most of the bays have been dredged and filled. Further, urban areas gird the mouths of rivers and coastal estuaries. Urbanization has many indirect impacts, coming from the demands it places on forests for wood production, on farms for food production, and on rivers for hydro production and flood control. In the coastal region, the impact of large dams on coho is less than in the Columbia, Snake, and Klamath River basins. However, forest, farm, and urban land use practices combine to encroach on coho habitat. Throughout their life cycle, coho fall prey to human activities accentuated by natural processes.

## Values

Valuing coho mostly as a commodity and emphasizing the community income generated from commercial and recreational fishing contributed to the coho decline. Greater production of salmon was believed to result in greater value to society. People understood that natural systems were limited, so hatcheries were developed. Hatchery salmon temporarily increased productivity by reducing juvenile mortality and producing more salmon for anglers and commercial fishers. Further, it was believed that hatcheries could substitute productivity for habitat lost to forestry, farming, and urbanization. As hatchery technology developed, it was used more and more broadly.

Science was pressed into use to improve hatchery production and to maximize the use of naturally spawning stocks. Using the concept of maximum sustainable yield, biologists sought to determine the maximum number of salmon that could be caught while maintaining the breeding population necessary to perpetuate the runs. When problems occurred and production did not meet expectations, coastal communities noted their resource dependence and claimed change would cause economic disadvantage. They were indeed weaker than urban centers whose economies were less dependent on natural resources. Suggestions to reduce forest extraction and agricultural development to protect salmon were resisted by coastal community leaders who felt that without a growing timber industry, expanding fisheries, and more productive agriculture, the economic well-being of the entire region would decline. Therefore, the management of salmon was complicated by an imperative to grow economically.

Meanwhile, a countervailing set of values, oriented toward protecting the environment in the face of economic expansion, was gaining strength. With the passage of the Endangered Species Act (ESA) in 1973, conservationists had acquired a powerful tool for protecting species at risk of extinction. In 1990 several Northwest organizations concerned about the widespread declines of salmonid populations began petitioning for their protection. In 1993, conservation groups filed petitions to protect coho under the ESA, and threats of additional legal measures to protect coho further constrained fishery managers.

The first petitions, designed to protect chinook and sockeye salmon on the Columbia and Snake Rivers, attracted the attention of powerful political and economic interests. Agricultural, barging, aluminum manufacturing, and electricity-generation firms trumpeted the economic costs of protecting salmon and the likely damage to their industries if the Columbia system were changed. The potential consequences of major change to allowed uses of the Columbia-Snake River system, the crucial economic artery for the noncoastal Northwest, were too great to ignore. As a result, by 1993, a broad cross section of regional society had been exposed to the issues surrounding salmon protection. By 1991, Snake River sockeye had received ESA protection, and in 1992 Snake River fall chinook were protected under the ESA, so the petitions that arose on coastal coho came with local precedent. The coastwide scope of the petitions, and their potential effects on small communities dependent on resource extraction, meant an intensifying contest between the traditional values associated with resource extraction and the emergent values favoring conservation.

## Lessons Learned

The first lesson learned from this complicated history is that the coho closure resulted from the complex interaction of many factors, including overreliance on hatcheries, changed natural conditions, and incomplete and inaccurate scientific knowledge. The natural variability of stocks and the incompleteness of scientific knowledge made it difficult to argue for reduced fishing—how could managers be sure that what they were saying was correct? The uncertainty that led to overfishing was not illegal, but resulted in harvest rates being set too high. By the time the scientific evidence was clear enough to take action, coho had declined precipitously.

Second, regulatory events predicted the closure. Increasingly specific and restrictive rules focused on protecting more and more stocks and restricted who could fish in each area and for how long. The management process became increasingly costly, burdensome, and time consuming. Despite these efforts, stocks continued to decline.

Third, the problems in the salmon fishery led to difficulties for those who still fished. The number of recreational fishers declined significantly; ocean recreational coho fishing is restricted to hook and release, although hatchery interests propose rebuilding the fishery by allowing catch of hatchery coho, with wild coho being released. Such a fishery is possible because all hatchery coho are fin clipped for identification purposes. In the commercial fishery, professional trollers switched to long-lining for bottom fish, trolling for albacore, fishing in other areas, and finding other jobs to supplement their fishing incomes. Large numbers of retirees and part-timers left the commercial fishery. Tribal fishers, who won equal shares with nontribal fishers in the 1970s and who were moving toward a 50-50 division, found that their catch levels were often less than when they had been allocated just 5 percent of the catch.

Fourth, it has become clear that measuring the success of fisheries solely on production has contributed to the problem. New approaches to management recognize the importance of naturally spawning stocks, ocean conditions, ocean and terrestrial habitats, and stock mixing. Because chinook and coho intermingle, management has to consider both. Fishery managers cannot directly control land use practices, but through endangered species and water-quality requirements, forest, farm, and urban land uses and their impacts on fish stocks are receiving more attention.

Fifth, the watershed has become the focal unit for community action on habitat restoration. In 1992, the Oregon legislature passed legislation to encourage the formation of watershed councils. By the end of 1997, all coastal watersheds had been included in a watershed council. California, Oregon, and Washington passed funding to support councils, which also were able to secure funding from private and federal agencies to augment programs. In 1998, the Conservation Reserve Enhancement Program committed $500 million to Washington and Oregon for a period of 15 years. Some successes from the efforts of watershed councils are being reported.[24]

Sixth, regional priorities, government actions, agency rhetoric, and the behavior of fishers are changing. Washington, Oregon, and California are developing innovative approaches to restoring salmon and are committing state resources to fund them. In 1993, Oregon created a Watershed Health Program (ORS 541). The same year Washington created the Jobs for the Environment Program, and a year later, the Washington Watershed Restoration Partnership Program received funding. In 1997, the California legislature funded a $40 million, five-year habitat restoration program. Oregon completed an innovative restoration plan in 1997 called the Oregon Plan for Salmon and Watersheds.[25] The 1997 Oregon legislature authorized a timber tax of $30 million over two years to fund the plan. The Washington Department of Fish and Wildlife (WDFW) admitted that its management of fisheries had been too production oriented and in 1997 developed new policies to emphasize naturally spawning salmon and rely less on hatchery production. The WDFW Salmonid Policy protects native stocks and natural production, gives priority to threatened and endangered stocks, and seeks to maintain self-sustaining populations.[26] The 1998 Washington legislature appropriated a level of funding to programs for salmon enhancement comparable to that of Oregon and California.

Finally, with salmon getting considerable media attention, the public has become much more concerned about their future. Several recent surveys show the importance of salmon in the Pacific Northwest.[27] In several surveys, people were asked whether they agreed or disagreed with the statement "Greater protection should be given to fish and wildlife habitats." A strong majority of people in the Pacific Northwest agreed and strongly agreed (figure 3).[28] A University of Idaho study found that protecting water and watersheds ranked higher than recreation, wilderness, and ecosystems.[29]

Salmon management has moved from a focus on single species, production levels, and volume of catch to healthy habitats and ecosystems, the escapement of naturally spawning stocks, and the interconnectedness of natural processes. Four years is too short a time to know if this will change the long-term pattern of salmon decline. Human expansion and destruction of salmon habitats continue. Whether the course toward decline changes depends on how important salmon really are to the culture of the Pacific Northwest.

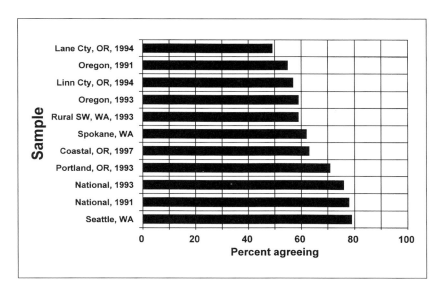

*Figure 3. Support for protecting salmon.*

# Notes

1. Henry O. Wendler, 1966, *Regulation of Commercial Fishing Gear and Seasons on the Columbia River from 1859 to 1963,* Fisheries Research Papers of the Washington Department of Fisheries 2, no. 4 (Olympia: Washington Department of Fisheries).

2. Pacific Fishery Management Council, 1978, *Final Environmental Impact Statement and Fishery Management Plan for Commercial and Recreational Salmon Fisheries off the Coasts of Washington, Oregon, and California Commencing in 1978* (Portland: Pacific Fishery Management Council), i.

3. Jim Lichatowich, 1997, Evaluating Salmon Management Institutions: The Importance of Performance Measures, Temporal Scales, and Production Cycles, pp. 69–87 in Deanna J. Stouder, Peter A. Bisson, and Robert J. Naiman, eds., *Pacific Salmon and Their Ecosystems: Status and Future Options* (New York: Chapman and Hall).

4. James A. Lichatowich and John D. McIntyre, 1987, Use of Hatcheries in the Management of Pacific Anadromous Salmonids, *American Fisheries Society Symposium* 1:131–136; Columbia River Inter-Tribal Fish Commission, 1992, *Salmon Recovery Program for the Columbia Basin* (Portland, OR: Columbia River Inter-Tribal Fish Commission); Ray Hilborn, 1992, Hatcheries and the Future of Salmon in the Northwest, *Fisheries* 17(1): 5–8; Angelo Incerpi, 1996, Hatchery-Bashing: a Useless Pastime, *Fisheries* 21(5): 28; National Research Council (NRC), 1996, Hatcheries, pp. 302–323 in *Upstream: Salmon and Society in the Pacific Northwest* (Washington, D.C.: National Academy Press).

5. Pacific Fishery Management Council (PFMC), 1997, *Draft Amendment 13 to the Pacific Coast Salmon Plan* (Portland, OR: Pacific Fishery Management Council), 17.

6. T. E. Nickelson, J. W. Nicholas, A. M. McGie, R. B. Lindsay, D. L. Bottom, F. J. Kaiser, and S. E. Jacobs, 1992, *Status of Anadromous Salmonids in Oregon Coastal Basins* (Portland, OR: Oregon Department of Fish and Wildlife).

7. NRC 1996, 146–155.

8. NRC 1996, 305–314.

9. D. R. Steward and T. C. Bjornn, 1990, Supplementation of Salmon and Steelhead Stocks with Hatchery Fish: a Synthesis of Published Literature, Part 2, in. W. H. Miller, ed., *Analysis of Salmon and Steelhead Supplementation,* Parts 1–3. Technical Report 90–1 (Portland, OR: U.S. Department of Energy, Bonneville Power Administration).

10. El Niño begins in the south central Pacific Ocean and brings warm water, poor upwelling, and reduced chlorophyll off the Oregon and Washington coasts.

11. William G. Pearcy, 1992, *Ocean Ecology of North Pacific Salmonids* (Seattle: University of Washington Press, Washington Sea Grant); William G. Pearcy, 1997, Salmonid Production in Changing Ocean Domains, pp. 331–352 in Deanna J. Stouder, Peter A. Bisson, and Robert J. Naiman, eds., *Pacific Salmon and Their Ecosystems: Status and Future Options* (New York: Chapman and Hall).

12. J. F. Palmisano, R. H. Ellis, and V. W. Kaczynski, 1993, *The Impact of Environmental and Management Factors on Washington's Wild Anadromous Salmon and Trout* (Olympia: Washington Forest Protection Association and Washington Department of Natural Resources); D. L. Park, 1993, *Transportation as a Means of Increasing Wild Juvenile Salmon Survival, Recovery Issues for Threatened and Endangered Snake River Salmon* (Portland, OR: U.S. Department of Energy, Bonneville Power Administration).

13. Nickelson et al. 1992.

14. Randy Henry, 1997, Fish and Wildlife on a Budget, *Oregon Wildlife Magazine* 54(2): 12–14; Thomas Heberlein, Quotations in Corvallis Gazette-Times, November 28, 1997, p. A7.

15. PMFC 1997, p. 17.

16. Pacific Fishery Management Council, 1997, *Review of 1996 Ocean Salmon Fisheries* (Portland, OR: Pacific Fishery Management Council), A-23; Pacific Fishery Management Council, 1993, *Historical Ocean Salmon Fishery Data for Washington, Oregon, and California* (Portland, OR: Pacific Fishery Management Council), W-129, O-51, and C-45.

17. Chris Carter, Oregon Department of Fish and Wildlife, personal communication.

18. Pacific Fishery Management Council, 1997, Salmon Management, *Council News* 21(4): 8.

19. Pacific Fishery Management Council, 2000, *Review of 1999 Ocean Salmon Fisheries* (Portland, OR: Pacific Fishery Management Council).

20. Washington Department of Fish and Wildlife and Oregon Department of Fish and Wildlife, 1996, *Status Report of Columbia River Fish Runs and Fisheries, 1938–1995* (Portland, OR: Oregon Department of Fish and Wildlife).

21. Washington Department of Fish and Wildlife, 1997, *Washington Salmon License Buy Out Program. Final Report,* Financial Assistance Award #NA66F10433.

22. D. B. Botkin, K. Cummins, T. Duune, H. Regier, M. Sobel, L. Talbot, and L. Simpson, 1995, *Status and Future of Salmon of Western Oregon and Northern California: Overview of Findings and Options,* Research Report 951002 (Santa Barbara, CA: Center for the Study of the Environment).

23. Shannon W. Davis and Hans D. Radtke, 1994, *A Demographic and Economic Description of the Oregon Coast* (Newport, OR: Oregon Coastal Zone Management Association), III-37.

24. W. F. Hudson and P. A. Heikkila, 1997, Integrating Public and Private Restoration Strategies: Coquille River of Oregon, pp. 233–250 in J. E. Williams, C. A. Wood, and M. P. Dombeck, eds., *Watershed Restoration: Principles and Practices* (Bethesda, MD: American Fisheries Society); *Restoration,* a newsletter published by Oregon Sea Grant.

25. http://www.oregon-plan.org/

26. John Harrison, 1997, Where Salmon Are Clients, Not Products, *Northwest Energy News* 16(3): 28–30.

27. Martilla and Kiley, 1994, *Mid-Columbia Public Utility Districts Public Opinion Survey. Public Affairs Report and Action Plan* (Boston, MA: Martilla and Kiley); Oregon Progress Board and State Office of Economic Analysis, 1996, *Oregon Population Survey* (Salem, OR: Oregon Progress Board and State Office of Economic Analysis).

28. M. Brunson and B. S. Steel, 1994, National Public Attitudes Toward Federal Rangeland Management, *Rangelands* 16: 77–81; B. S. Steel, P. List, B. Shindler, and C. Smith, 1994, *Survey of Forestry Issues in Lane and Linn Counties* (Vancouver, WA: Washington State University); Shindler, B., P. List, C. Smith, and B. S. Steel, 1995, *Initial Social Assessment of Proximate Communities: Central Cascades Adaptive Management Area. Cascade Center for Ecosystem Management* (Corvallis, OR: USDA Forest Service).

29. G. Rudzitis, C. Watrous, and H. Johansen, 1995, *Public Views on Public Lands: A Survey of Interior Columbia Basin Residents* (Moscow, ID: University of Idaho Department of Geography).

# CHAPTER 10

# Compensating for Losses During Pacific Salmon Fishery Crises

*R. Bruce Rettig*

## Introduction

Concerns about both social equity and economic efficiency trigger a public debate over who should bear the costs of salmon decline and recovery.[1] Three threads are woven into these discussions; each links to other social debates. When should society compensate for diminished private property rights? When, how, and how much should society compensate for losses caused by natural hazards? What role should society play in the reduction of fishing fleet capacity? I'll look first at the question of property rights.

## Regulatory Takings

The Fifth Amendment of the U.S. Constitution ends with the words "nor shall private property be taken for public use, without just compensation." And the Fourteenth Amendment tells us that "No State shall make or enforce any law which shall abridge the privileges or immunities of citizens of the United States; nor shall any State deprive any person of life, liberty, or property, without due process of law; nor deny to any person within its jurisdiction the equal protection of the laws." In the 1922 landmark Supreme Court decision *Pennsylvania Coal v. Mahon*, regulations that stripped property of all value were also deemed to violate the takings restrictions identified in the Bill of Rights. In recent years, courts and legislatures have worried about regulations that reduce the value of property without total elimination of market value.

What does this have to do with the salmon crisis? Several environmental laws have been attacked for taking private property rights without providing just compensation. Congress and many state legislatures have dealt with legislation that would award compensation for diminished property values caused by environmental protection.

Two major arguments work against uniform and complete requirements for compensation. The first is the common law of nuisance. We widely accept that a property owner should not store toxic wastes when those wastes leach into groundwater or otherwise harm public health and safety. Whether protection of endangered species, wetlands, and other natural habitat features is part of public nuisance law is largely left up to state law. The second counterargument comes from the public trust doctrine. In short, some rights may not be subject to takings because they never belonged to the property owner. Although rights are primarily a matter of equity, economic arguments are relevant to their treatment as well.

Consider that the value to society of restoring salmon habitat on a parcel of privately owned land exceeds the value to the property owner of development. If the landowner does not have the legal right to carry out the development, the development should be restricted.[2] However, if she does have the right, compensation will be a useful incentive for conservation. An appropriate amount of compensation would be the value of the protected habitat to society. However, economists do not have sufficiently credible techniques for estimating this value, so "fair market value" is a compromise.[3] The Oregon Coastal Salmon Restoration Initiative includes many references to compensation, largely in terms of incentives and in-kind assistance with restoration.

The first step in making compensation judgments should begin with a determination that the benefits of an environmental policy exceed its costs. Because economists widely agree that they cannot estimate the full value of salmon protection measures, we must draw upon a social judgment that the action is worth its costs and then select the measures providing the most cost-effective procedure to achieve the recovery goals. In short, with limited budgets, good biological advice is needed to get the biggest bang for the buck.

Assuming that the regulation is efficient in this sense, the next step is to determine demoralization costs (the full range of consequences from not providing compensation).[4] The most common example is underinvestment, as when a landowner cuts her forest when it is still young because she fears a loss of future harvest revenues and no compensation for the lost revenue.

Finally, there are settlement costs (all the costs from awarding compensation). These costs include not only the funds given out and the administrative costs to carry out compensation, but also any indirect losses, such as wasteful investments, that are undertaken because full compensation for any improvement is expected later.

Compensation should be paid if the net efficiency gains exceed settlement costs and settlement costs are less than demoralization costs. Compensation is not economically efficient when demoralization costs are less than settlement costs. One way to frame this is to recognize that tax dollars provided in compensation demoralize the taxpayer. In summary, compensation for real or perceived lost development values on private land provides incentives to make productive investments while preserving environmental values that exceed development values.

Headlines in the Portland *Oregonian* on August 24, 1997 suggested that $3 billion spent on salmon protection in the Columbia River basin has done little good. Unless new accountability procedures do a better job, the entire salmon protection process may begin to unravel. This suggests that the work of biologists to identify the most effective salmon protection strategies and to articulate those strategies to the public is critical. Also, unless dramatic successes unfold quickly, strategies that diminish the value of privately owned land may need to provide more compensation to those who bear the costs.

Two recent regulatory takings decisions from the U.S. Supreme Court involve natural hazards. *Lucas v. South Carolina Coastal Council* involved a refusal by the South Carolina Coastal Council of a building permit for undeveloped properties seaward of an erosion setback baseline. *Dolan v. City of Tigard* involved requirements by the city of Tigard, Oregon, that a property owner dedicate a portion of her land within a 100-year floodplain to the city and also that Dolan provide an additional 15-foot strip adjoining the floodplain to be used as part of the city's pedestrian and bikeway system. After analyzing these and several other cases, Platt and Dawson conclude that property owners cannot use their property to the detriment of themselves, their neighbors, or the general public, but that the public cannot compel property owners to bear a disproportionate burden of the cost of public goals.[5] They also emphasize that compensation for natural hazard mitigation has several features that separate it from regulations that have a more general purpose of maintaining ecological integrity. This leads to the second theme of this paper: why, where, and when do we compensate victims of natural hazards? And are there lessons for adaptations to what first looked like a brief, but intense, El Niño and now appears to be part of longer cycles?

## Natural Hazards

If at all possible, damages from natural hazards are to be prevented. When this is not possible, the next highest priority is to mitigate the impact of the natural hazard. Hazard insurance programs play a valuable role in enlisting the affected parties in mitigation actions and in spreading the burden of damages. Compensation to victims for uninsured damages is important but should be the last step in this process of prevention, mitigation, and compensation.

Blume, Rubinfeld, and Shapiro proved that compensation provides the same incentives to a landowner as insurance.[6] People buy insurance to protect their investments against uncertain events. When risky outcomes are predictable, it makes sense to allow people to purchase insurance. However, some risky outcomes are highly unpredictable. In those cases, society can provide the equivalent of a group insurance fund by providing compensation equivalent to the insured coverage we would have chosen had we known that there was a probability of an adverse outcome. All pay taxes to provide this level of social protection.

The key is predictability. When floods in the Mississippi River created record damage, social acceptance of relief was wide. However, circumstances change when scientists predict significant probability of additional damage. If people rebuild in floodplains, the economic advice is that property owners should acquire actuarially fair insurance. If private insurance is not forthcoming and there is a public interest in resettlement, public insurance or partial compensation may be in order.

Disaster relief for changes in ocean environmental conditions shares many of the sources and consequences of other disaster relief programs. The fishing industry did not insure itself fully, but this is similar to other cases. Many residents of southern California do not purchase earthquake insurance, making building and zoning requirements essential. Similarly, residents of Florida underinsure for hurricanes, and residents of the Mississippi floodplain lack enough flood insurance.

Floods and droughts are familiar applications of this reasoning. What is less conventional is the assertion that changing ocean conditions play a major role in fish stock declines. On the basis of that presumption, Congress reasoned that ocean conditions are unpredictable (or, at least, were not predicted in a probabilistic sense) and that the same sort of disaster relief available for floods and hurricanes be extended to people in the salmon industry. Much of the recent El Niño relief was fairly conventional, especially in the Gulf of Mexico, where it was tied to floods and other extreme storm events. However, in New England and in the Pacific salmon fishery, relief was tied closely to concerns about reduction in fishing capacity. That is to say, just as some flood relief was followed by measures to avoid future building in the floodplain, the relief in New England and Pacific states was designed to avoid a repetition of unfortunate circumstances.

## Reduction in Fishing Capacity

Why have so many programs to reduce fishing capacity appeared recently all over the world? Many financially distressed people plan to retire, change fisheries, or seek another occupation, not because they want to do so, but because they despair of recent experiences. At least some in the fishing industry believe that those wishing to stay in the industry would stand a better chance at economic survival if a portion of their fleet were bought out. A second force comes from outside the industry. It reflects a growing concern of the public that the decline of some fish stocks is caused, at least in part, by overfishing and that a smaller fishing industry would be more likely to accept sustainable fishing practices and take chances with weak stocks than would the current industry.[7]

The Washington Salmon License Buyout Program arose from recent disaster relief efforts. Its first objective was to provide short-term relief to as many people as possible who were suffering economic losses from depressed salmon stocks. Several people did receive compensation. Approximately 40 percent of the 668 salmon troll licenses eligible for 1995 renewal were bought out in the two programs. Activity in Columbia River gill-net licenses and salmon charter licenses was lower, with 27 percent of the 506 gill-net licenses and 16 percent of the charter licenses being bought. After the first round of buyouts through the Northwest Emergency Assistance Program, but before the second round went into effect, Gilden and Smith surveyed Oregon and Washington gillnetters about their buyback program.[8] In response to their question," Did you get what you needed from the disaster relief programs?" 11 percent said yes, 75 percent said no, and 13 percent gave indeterminate responses. Although many license holders have received some relief, many felt they were entitled to much more compensation. Frustration remains high.

The second objective of the Washington Department of Fish and Wildlife (WDFW) program was to provide economic relief indirectly by aligning capacity closer to a figure that would provide good sustainable incomes. On the basis of public hearings, WDFW determined that the first round probably did retire many licenses from people who were not as actively involved as those remaining in the program. For this reason and because the more productive fishers felt they were effectively left out of the program, the focus of the program changed. On the second round, rather than buying licenses from those willing to accept the least amount of money, WDFW followed a formula that gave priority to those who submitted the lowest ratio of offer price to salmon impact. Salmon impact was defined as the difference between the highest gross salmon income derived from a designated salmon fishing activity during any calendar year from 1986 through 1991 and the sum of the least amount of gross income derived from the same salmon fishing activity during any calendar year from 1991 through 1995. Although the principal purpose of the change was to address equity concerns identified in public hearings, there was a hope that this second formula might have reduced fishing capacity more by removing more high-liners.

A third major objective was to create a more sustainable environment for the fishery. Given the continuing restrictions associated with low coho salmon populations, it may be a long time before the sustainable long-term future of this fishery, and the success of the program, can be adequately addressed.

Appraisals of other capacity reduction programs are striking, both in the care with which capacity reduction programs were analyzed and in the skepticism expressed that the programs have been helpful.[9] One major concern is with latent capacity, which refers to the fact that much of any licensed fleet includes vessels and licenses that provide little fishing effort, and these are the vessels and licenses most likely to be sold under a retirement plan.

Related to this problem are distortions in measures of capacity. Capacity is the expected harvest potential associated with a specific vessel or license. If fewer licenses are found in a fishery, each is likely to provide more fishing effort. To some extent, controlling some measures of a fishing vessel, such as length or hold capacity, can offset this. However, shipyards have shown an amazing ability to increase the effectiveness of vessels within limited specifications. Gates and his coauthors report research showing that fishing power has risen over time with technological advances and suggest that this is likely to continue to be the case.[10]

## Summary and Conclusions

Considerations of both equity and economic efficiency suggest that compensation is a valuable tool in the restoration of salmon habitat and in salmon fishery management. On the other hand, equity may limit compensation and favor in-kind over cash compensation. Economic efficiency also limits compensation when it causes distortions and creates incentives to undertake wasteful investments and cause indirect harm. History suggests that compensation for landowners is likely to become more rather than less important over time.

Compensation for disaster relief is a form of social insurance for unpredicted natural phenomena that cause large losses. Although recurring natural hazards could, in theory, be treated through private insurance, limited information and cognitive biases often lead to underinsurance. In these cases, programs that mitigate the need for future relief may be warranted.

One form of mitigation against economic losses in fisheries is fleet capacity reduction. These programs reflect attempts by the fishing industry to restructure itself into a sustainable form. They also reflect a social impatience with a perceived global crisis in marine fisheries and the need to take a wide range of measures to avoid recent trends.

Finally, those who care about salmon and the people who harvest salmon face enough problems addressing the technical research questions of biology and physical processes. Fair compensation, including in-kind measures and other rewards for helpful landowners and harvesters, can remove some of the noise and exasperation seen by the public and let society get on with business.

## Notes

1. H. Berry and R. B. Rettig, 1994, *Who Should Pay for Salmon Recovery?* Pacific Cooperative Extension publication PNW-470.

2. If the value of the development exceeds the preservation value, society has the opportunity, but not an obligation, to grant development rights.

3. Compensation for landowners is discussed in S. Polasky, H. Doremus, and R. B. Rettig, 1997, Endangered Species Conservation on Private Land, *Contemporary Economic Policy* 15.

4. The use of the words "demoralization" and "settlement" comes from Frank I. Michelman, 1967, Property, Utility, and Fairness: Comments on the Ethical Foundations of "Just Compensation" Law, *Harvard Law Review* 80: 1165–1258.

5. Rutherford H. Platt and Alexandra D. Dawson, 1997, *The Taking Issue and the Regulation of Hazardous Areas,* Natural Hazards Research Working Paper #95 (Boulder, CO: Natural Hazards Research and Applications Information Center, Institute of Behavioral Science, University of Colorado).

6. Lawrence E. Blume, Daniel L. Rubinfeld, and Perry Shapiro, 1984, The Taking of Land: When Should Compensation be Paid? *Quarterly Journal of Economics* 99: 71–92.

7. See, for example, Pamela Mace, 1997, Developing and Sustaining World Fisheries Resources: The State of the Science and Management, pp. 1–22 in D. A. Hancock, D. C. Smith, A. Grant, and J. P. Beumer. *Developing and Sustaining World Fisheries Resources: The State of the Science and Management* (Collingwood, Victoria, Australia: CSIRO Publishing).

8. Jennifer Gilden and Courtland Smith, 1996, *Survey of Gillnetters in Oregon and Washington: Summary of Results* (Corvallis, OR: Oregon Sea Grant).

9. See the following works and citations in each of these works: Rögnvaldur Hannesson, 1996, *Fisheries Mismanagement: The Case of the North Atlantic Cod* (Cambridge, MA: Fishing News Books); William Schrank, 1997, The Newfoundland Fishery: Past, Present, and Future, pp. 35–70 in Scott Burns, ed., *Subsidies and Depletion of World Fisheries* (Washington, D.C.: World Wildlife Fund); and John Gates, Dan Holland, and Eyjolfur Gudmundsson, 1997, Theory and Practice of Fishing Vessel Buyback Programs, pp. 71–117 in Scott Burns, ed., *Subsidies and Depletion of World Fisheries* (Washington, D.C.: World Wildlife Fund).

10. Gates et al. 1997.

# Integrating Research, Outreach, and Communication

## CHAPTER 11

# Using Collaborative Problem-Solving Process in Fisheries Management Decisions

*Rollie Barnaby*

## Background

In New England most people would agree the fisheries management system has not maintained marine fish stocks to adequate levels. Even the fishing industry has gone beyond the denial period and agrees. We cannot put the blame on fisheries science, fishers, or fisheries managers. All the parties responsible for fisheries management in New England worked diligently and sincerely, but they worked alone. The solutions presented by scientists were rejected by the managers, the solutions put forward by managers were rejected by fishers, the fishers' solutions were rejected by the conservationists, and the circle continues.

One of the positive things to come out of the fisheries collapse is a heightened interest in learning about different management systems. The fishing industry seems to be most interested in any management that revolves around its participation, such as co-management, bottom-up management, self-management, and community-based management. Fishers are indicating that providing input at public hearings and council meetings is not enough. Unfortunately, most fishers don't appreciate how much work it will require to be part of a true participatory management system. As a result, the Maine Fishermen's Forum and the Gloucester Fishermen's Forum, both multiday events and the best-attended fishers' meetings in New England, have held several sessions on participatory management systems.

## Lobster Councils

The State of Maine started a participatory management system in the lobster fishery by passing legislation in 1995 that created discrete management zones recognizing that fishing practices vary significantly from one area of the coastline to the next because of differences in geography, benthic habitat, custom, and shoreside economic conditions. The legislation empowers lobstermen of each zone to

- negotiate their boundaries with neighboring zones
- set trap limits that are less than current law
- set limits on time or days of fishing that are more restrictive than current law
- manage restrictions on the number of traps used on trawls

Each zone has an elected council, each of whose members represents 70 to 100 fishers. Changes in regulations specific to a zone must be ratified by a two-thirds vote in a referendum ballot mailed to all license holders in that zone. This is the first real attempt in this region to allow fishers to make binding management decisions. The regulations that fishers have been given control of are limited, but this is still an important step in developing a participatory management structure.

The biggest criticism of the Maine Zone Council system has been that other important stakeholders have been left out of the process. How does science enter into the decision-making process? What about other marine users, such as recreational boaters, and other fishing gear types? How do conservation organizations give their input? Where do the lobster dealers and consumers fit into the decision making? How about towns, marina operators, and marine trades? These other stakeholders might not be needed for the types of decisions being made now, but I believe they will have to be included if more jurisdiction is going to be given to the lobster fishermen. How then do we handle differences in opinions or regulations between zones?

## Harbor Porpoise Work Group

I believe that management decisions should involve all the relevant and affected parties, or stakeholders. The process should be as inclusive as possible. One of the experiences that led me to this belief was my work with a group that got together in response to a situation in which marine mammals were being caught in gill nets. The Harbor Porpoise Working Group was an ad hoc group that met voluntarily with no authority or mandate. It consisted of fishers, scientists, representatives of environmental organizations, fisheries managers, fishing gear experts, and an extension educator. The group met on a regular basis for almost five years.

This was the most exciting, frustrating, difficult, rewarding, and educational project I have ever been involved with. We spent a year without making any progress, arguing about porpoise populations, numbers of takes, the value of marine mammals, and the effects of gill nets. It wasn't until the group agreed on a goal that some progress was made. The goal was to reduce the take of harbor porpoise with the least impact possible on the fishing industry. The next important lesson we learned was that there were certain things the group would never agree on, such as porpoise population estimates and the number of porpoise takes. To make progress, we had to put aside those differences. The group had to find those things they did agree on and go from there.

Then the group looked for creative solutions. The obvious solution was to close down the fishery, but that wasn't acceptable to the fishers and certainly didn't meet the goal of seeking action that had "the least impact on the fishing industry." The most appealing solutions revolved around some kind of gear modification. Someone in the group had heard about work that Dr. Jon Lien from Newfoundland, Canada, was doing to keep humpback whales out of cod traps. His approach was to put a noisemaker (pinger) on the cod traps that indicated to the whales that something was there. Most acoustical devices that had been used to change an animal's behavior up to this time were obnoxious noisemakers meant to scare away the animal. Dr. Lien's pinger did not scare the animals; it just made the trap or net more visible acoustically.

Dr. Lien came to New Hampshire and helped fishers conduct trials using pingers to keep harbor porpoise from running into the gill nets. The results were very promising and the fishers were convinced they worked. It was the Harbor Porpoise Working Group that pushed the concept forward, even though some of the scientists and environmentalists were skeptical. I don't believe the concept would have gotten off the drawing boards if this group hadn't been working together.

The New England gillnetters are now using pingers on their gill nets during the time when harbor porpoise are migrating through their area. The pingers were found to reduce take by as much as 90 percent in an experiment conducted in 1995. Pingers are now being used around the world in other applications, reducing the take of seabirds in nets and the number of marine mammals caught in shark nets in Australia.

This was a collaborative problem-solving exercise, but the participants did not realize it at the time. The most important result for me was a new belief in the power of collaborative problem solving. I was convinced that the harbor porpoise project would have been much less painful and taken less time if the participants had had some knowledge and experience in collaborative problem solving. We might have worked on a goal much sooner, and we would have known that there is a difference between a person's position and his or her interest. The group might have looked for common ground sooner by identifying those things they could not agree on early in the process.

As a result of this experience I have received training in and studied the process of collaborative problem solving. In partnership with the Conservation Law Foundation, I conducted a one-day workshop in 1994 for 20 people involved in fisheries management. After a couple of years I realized some of the participants were having a big effect on fisheries management using the information they received at our workshop. Last year I received a NMFS Saltonstall/Kennedy grant to conduct seven one-day workshops around New England on collaborative decision making for fishers.

If a truly participatory fisheries management system is going to be successful in New England, I believe these collaborative decision-making skills are going to be extremely important. One of the facilitators who helped organize the Maine Lobster Zone Councils called me recently to ask about the workshops because he had seen the need while organizing the zone councils.

## Northwest Atlantic Marine Alliance

For the past three years I have been working with a group of fishers, fisheries leaders, the Conservation Law Foundation, and Dee Hock (retired CEO of VISA International) on investigating, designing, and now implementing a self-organizing and self-managing fisheries organization. The purpose of the Northwest Atlantic Marine Alliance (NAMA) is to create a community-based, self-organizing, and self-regulating organization to restore and enhance an enduring northwest Atlantic marine system that supports a healthy diversity and abundance of marine life and commercial, recreational, aesthetic, and other uses.

Guiding principles of the organization are that every part of NAMA shall

- be open to all individuals and institutions that fully subscribe to the organization's purpose and principles

- have the right to organize in any manner, at any scale, in any area, and around any issue or activity that is relevant to and consistent with the purpose of the organization
- vest authority in and make decisions at the most local level that includes all relevant and affected parties

We can see how NAMA differs from traditional organizational structures. The organizing committee has identified eight categories of membership that are necessary for NAMA to operate: fixed-gear fishers, mobile-gear fishers, aquaculturists, allied industries (processors, equipment suppliers, wholesalers), recreational users (fishers, boaters, scuba divers), commercial recreational (whale watching, charter boats), research-education, and conservation-environmental. A ninth category would also be welcome: government.

NAMA has received over $50,000 from foundations to start up this organization. The organizing committee has developed the purpose and principles and has the concept and structure 75 percent developed. It is now in the process of formally incorporating and applying for charitable status under the federal code. The next major effort will be to engage fishers and other marine users in discussions about NAMA and participatory management systems.

I believe for fisheries management to be effective, some form of participatory system will have to be in place. From my experience of talking with industry members, I know that many New England fishers are ready to take part. Participatory management will create the sense of ownership needed for compliance to take place in fisheries. Worldwide experience has shown that no matter how perfect the fishery management system seems to the scientist or manager, if it is not acceptable to fishers, the chances of success are very limited.

The diversity of fishers, fishing strategies, species, gear types, and geography cannot be taken into account in a centralized, top-down management structure. Local knowledge and collective wisdom is also lost in a centralized structure as well as active and open critical analysis. Fishers and other users have the potential to add to the knowledge and database used in making management decisions. A true participatory system is needed because advisory and co-managed groups are often co-opted by government bureaucrats, politicians, and stronger industry groups in centralized systems.

I believe institutional change occurs in small steps rather than through radical innovations or total reorganization. Any new approach will take time, but the fisheries crisis unfolding in New England and around the world today may help speed up the process.

# CHAPTER 12

## The Audience as Co-producer: Experiments in Public Outreach Communications

### *Joseph Cone*

Throughout the familiar saying "The pen is mightier than the sword" serves as a reminder that communication is a tool to create change. Professional communicators—writers, editors, and other specialists—appreciate this adage and nominally intend to create some sort of change, in attitudes, knowledge, or behavior, whenever they communicate. Nevertheless, communicators who work in government agencies and in higher education are often limited in their effectiveness in communicating with the public. Usually the causes are a distant, superficial relationship with their audiences, worsened by a simplistic one-way-flow model of communications.

To play off the memorable quotation from the movie *Field of Dreams,* the assumption in such cases seems to be that "If you say it, they will listen." Much too frequently, public affairs or public information people seem to believe that their role is "to get the word out" about a particular institutional program. Yes, but is anybody listening? Do the supposed listeners care about what is being said? Is the method of presentation itself putting them off? Also, there is a sort of free market attitude in agencies about getting out information. They assume that facts alone lead to "correct" private and civic decisions.

Confusion about the role of communicators employed by public agencies is reflected in the words commonly used to describe the people for whom our information services are intended. The language of commerce is much in vogue in government and education today. We speak of "customers," but are we seriously considering treating people the way capitalist business sometimes treats its customers, as the necessary engine of profits? "Clientele" is also fashionable but may be little more than cant; one wonders how much we are really working for the clientele. Even the hallowed term "audience" evokes a contrary metaphor: do we see ourselves as performers, running off our lines before a captive audience?

So, what term would be preferable? Canadian philosopher John Ralston Saul notes this "tendency to refer to the citizen as a customer of the government . . . [b]ut we [citizens] are not customers. We haven't walked into a shop to think about buying. . . .We are the owners of the services in question. . . . Not only are we not the customers of public servants, we are in fact their employers."[1] As Saul suggests, we public-agency communicators need to remind ourselves that we're addressing not customers, not clientele, but our fellow citizens.

In the case of the Adapting to Change project (ATC), we knew we would be communicating primarily with members of fishing families. We had several resources to draw upon in our communications tasks. First, the ATC effort was designed so that the research and outreach faculty involved in the project could act as information resources for each other. All the faculty were at least acquainted with each other through regular meetings, and many of us had worked together before, in some instances over a period of years. In particular, the Extension Sea Grant agents, who live in coastal communities, could provide substantial direct information about the fishing industry and fishing communities to researchers and communicators. Finally, as the ATC projects were conducted, a significant body of new information about fishing families became available to all of us, including the communicators. For example, three opinion surveys were conducted in the first 18 months of ATC, which showed, among other things, that members of the fishing industry are rather suspicious of academics and government information sources.[2]

Since the purpose of ATC outreach was to help members of fishing families understand and adapt to economic, social, and environmental changes, we recognized the need to relate to them differently, to have them feel capable in the circumstances they found themselves in—in short, to empower them. Empowerment involves giving people access to powerful tools. We've done that in slightly different ways with three communications efforts. In all of them, Extension specialist Flaxen Conway, who led the outreach effort associated with ATC, played a significant role. The first two efforts, in fact, were initiated by her, and the Communications office had minor but contributing roles.

## Fishing Family Newsletters

Since 1995, fishing family coordinators have worked on ATC in Brookings, Newport, and Astoria, Oregon, towns located in the southern, central, and northern regions of the Oregon coast. During this time, the coordinators have produced short (eight pages or fewer), quarterly newsletters. Each publication has approximately 1,000 fishing community recipients, so a fair amount of locally produced information has been reaching about 3,000 people. Sea Grant's oversight of the newsletters has been deliberately restrained.

The newsletters are reviewed before publication by the cooperating Extension agents who supervised the fishing family coordinators. A very few editorial guidelines have been offered to the coordinators by Communications, passed along to the coordinators from Conway through the local agents. Meanwhile, the Sea Grant science writer has also forwarded progress reports of the research projects to the coordinators, fulfilling our early promises to keep fishing families informed about the projects.

Unlike most other newsletters supported by a government-funded program, these fishing family newsletters are not primarily written, edited, designed, or even approved by some central administrative office, such as Communications. Rather, the newsletters are viewed mainly as vehicles for the sharing of local knowledge as submitted by the fishing family coordinators and other community members. They are deliberately informal and noninstitutional in appearance.

## Letters to Fishing Families

Conway also arranged for a series of a dozen letters to be written by a writer who was formerly married to a commercial fisherman. The titles of two letters suggest the colloquial approach of the series: *When and How to Argue: A Fishing Family Dilemma* and *Helping Kids Understand What Daddy Does When He's Away*. The informal design of the publications was consistent with this approach.

Sea Grant Communications became involved in this project mainly in providing a technical edit of the letters. In editing, we tried to not lose sight of our main objectives of relevance and acceptance of the letters by the fishing family members, typically wives, to whom the letters were addressed. We sought to accommodate what the writer, this former member of the "audience," thought would be suitable for the readers, even though, in certain instances, we might have preferred different approaches to the subject or a different writing style or tone. Our judgment was that our appropriate role in this communications task of creating a positive change was to facilitate, not interfere, with the message.

No formal assessment of the letters and the results of taking this approach has been conducted, but anecdotal testimony from at least some fishing wives who received these letters indicates that the letters have been very useful and appreciated.

## Fishing Family Video

This project was a particular kind of documentary videotape made about the members, mainly wives, of some fishing families, in Newport, Oregon. Again, in this ATC communications project, we reconsidered and adjusted some of the standard practices associated with producing such a video. Conventionally, a documentary video about fishermen's wives would be produced either for or about them. The production team on this video took a different approach, producing the video with the subjects.

The two people involved in shooting the video were trained in anthropology. The videographer was an experienced professional filmmaker who was completing a master's degree at Oregon State University. The project assistant held a master's degree in applied anthropology and had a strong interest in video production. They wanted to explore what could be achieved in understanding and portraying the lives of fishing families through an interactive process.

In some respects this video is similar to ethnographic videos that attempt to describe the culture of their subjects' lives. The videomakers filmed the women going about their daily routines, taking care of home and children while their spouses were at sea fishing. After the footage was shot, the videographer viewed the footage with the fishing wives, asking them to help select footage that would tell a story about them that they thought was important. In this last step of reflection by the subjects, the video was intended to go beyond a more standard ethnographic approach.

Either an ethnographic or what might be called a "reflective-ethnographic" documentary, like this one, is substantially different from the conventional documentary or educational production funded by a third party, particularly a government-funded program. Conventionally, such a documentary or educational video would begin with a narration and a tightly identified message structure, determined by the producers. By contrast, in this case the story structure and narration came last and were developed by the Sea Grant staff writer. Instead, the goal of this video was to create a certain depth of understanding of these people holding a mirror up to themselves and then turning it around for others to see. We hoped that both the fishing families and those who interact with them, such as academics and regulatory officials, would benefit from the exposure.

This sort of reflective documentary may be more common in the future, not at least partly because the technology exists to produce such videos affordably. Historically, shooting video has been very expensive: perhaps $500 to $1,000 a day for an educational video. Editing and postproduction services have been even more expensive: commonly $200 an hour. Such costs have made producers wary of uncertainty or making changes. Making changes, however, is the essence of both the Adapting to Change video and the new world of nonlinear video editing.

Such nonlinear editing (editing done in a computer, with random access to program elements) makes it possible to move elements of a production around with a click of a computer mouse. In the dark ages of video editing—up until about 1993—editing was linear, much less flexible, and very tedious. Program segments were copied from source videotapes on to a master tape. Once elements were in place on the master, inserting changes was difficult and expensive.

With nonlinear editing, it was technically not difficult, for example, to videotape the participants as they commented on the scenes of themselves and insert those commentaries sequentially in video, as voice-over, or even as picture-in-picture commentaries.

All three of these projects, in different ways, were experiments in co-production. We worked with people who were the focus of our research and outreach attention, people some communicators might think of as a passive audience, as customers or clientele who are only going to learn and receive information from us. Quite to the contrary. We're learning, too, as we enrich the naive one-way communication model by empowering at least some of the receivers to be senders of information.

## Notes

1. John Ralston Saul, 1995, *The Unconscious Civilization* (Toronto: Anansi Press), p. 96.

2. Jennifer Gilden and Courtland Smith, 1996, *Survey of Gillnetters in Oregon and Washington: Summary of Results* (Corvallis, OR: Oregon Sea Grant); Jennifer

Gilden and Courtland Smith, 1996, *Survey of Oregon Troll Permit Owners: Summary of Results* (Corvallis, OR: Oregon Sea Grant); Courtland Smith, et al., 1997, *Oregon Coastal Salmon Restoration: Views of Coastal Residents* (Corvallis, OR: Oregon Sea Grant).

# CHAPTER 13

# Looking Back

*Jennifer Gilden and Jan Auyong*

## Introduction

Oregon Sea Grant's Adapting to Change (ATC) program was a multidisciplinary outreach and research effort that focused on fishing families, businesses, and communities in Oregon, Washington, California, and New England. The goal of the outreach project was to help fishing families, communities, and businesses adapt to changes in fisheries by responding to their immediate needs and building adaptation skills. The project involved a community development specialist, Extension field agents, fishing family coordinators, and communications staff. The research component involved such disciplines as anthropology, sociology, resource economics, human development and family sciences, and business administration. Research efforts investigated the economic history of New England and Pacific groundfish fisheries, the economic impacts of reduced harvests on Northwest and New England coastal communities, disaster relief programs for commercial salmon fishers, human capital in fishing communities, fishing family life and well-being, and disaster relief programming for ailing Pacific salmon fisheries.

Many of the participants hoped to create an interdisciplinary program from the ATC effort. As the project progressed, however, the impetus to integrate gradually faded or was thwarted. This paper presents lessons learned about attempting an interdisciplinary program. It does not propose to evaluate the effectiveness of the ATC research and outreach effort.

The discussion below focuses on barriers to integration as they relate to ATC.

In addition to reviewing program documents, we interviewed 12 of the 29 ATC project members about their perceptions of integration, in both the development and conduct of the program. Interviewees included researchers, Extension agents, graduate students, and administrative staff. Unless specifically stated, "Sea Grant" always refers to Oregon Sea Grant rather than the national Sea Grant program.

## Historical Context

In 1991, Oregon State University launched the Timber Dependent Families and Communities project, a university-wide, multidisciplinary program for the support of Oregon families and communities affected by the changing timber supply. The success of this project inspired several coastal Extension agents to contact the program's leader, a community development Extension specialist. Together, they proposed a related pilot project aimed at fishing families and communities dealing with declining resources and increasing regulation. The Fishing Dependent Families project was subsequently funded by Sea Grant in collaboration with the Oregon State University Extension Service in 1992.

The 18-month Fishing Dependent Families project was a community-based program for helping fishers and their families cope with social and economic changes affecting the commercial fishing industry. The project used three local peers (later called fishing family coordinators) at different locations along the coast. The pilot project's usefulness led to discussions of a larger project that would include a targeted research component, but finding sufficient funding was a challenge.

At that point, however, the national Sea Grant program was seeking proposals for a special enhancement initiative. The proposal schedule was very tight. Those involved with the Fishing Dependent Families project developed a list of possible collaborators, and the Sea Grant director invited interested researchers to an exploratory meeting in November 1994. At that meeting, the researchers shared their concepts or preliminary proposals. In December 1994 the researchers met with the Sea Grant director to discuss integration opportunities, overlap in the research, and industry involvement. A resource economics researcher and the Extension community development specialist then combined the seven individual proposed projects into a single package, which was submitted, reviewed, and funded in mid-1995.

Team members gathered several times at the beginning of the program to develop an organizational structure and a process for internal reporting or coordination. Ultimately, the group settled on remaining loosely organized, with coordination assistance provided by a member of Sea Grant administration. Quarterly meetings were to be held to report progress, coordinate logistics, or discuss constraints or interesting findings. A listserv mailing group was established by the coordinator to facilitate exchange of information, and the principal investigators of individual projects were encouraged to develop Web pages and interim briefing reports or publications.

Public informational workshops were also held in various coastal communities to introduce the program and its project members, identify potential problems or opportunities, coordinate research and fishing schedules, and obtain feedback on proposed activities. Audience members expressed a strong desire be kept informed about the research process and results, and the project members continue to feel a strong obligation to report their findings. Press releases and progress reports were supplied to local fishing organizations, such as fishermen's wives associations, to report on program activities.

In the first year of the program, interaction and enthusiasm among the members were high. However, as the main data-collection activities became more intense, members appeared to have fewer discussion items in common. As with many research projects, proposed tasks often took longer or required more effort than anticipated; and, as the months passed, project members became increasingly busy outside of the ATC program. As projects began to conclude, members tried to find common threads among their findings, often debating proposed themes and semantics. It was difficult to agree on products or activities in which to share project findings—for example, whether to hold a conference, develop a book, or create some other type of publication. Over time project members had drifted away from thinking about ATC as an integrated whole to being more focused on their own project and outcomes.

## Integrated and Multidisciplinary Research

Although the ATC project began as a multidisciplinary project, project members and Sea Grant administration still hoped for interdisciplinary outcomes. However, the structure and management of the project ultimately constrained the achievement of this goal. People often use the terms "interdisciplinary" and "multidisciplinary" interchangeably, creating confusion, particularly in the planning and implementation phases. Interdisciplinary work is generally defined as *integrated* work, that is, work "in which the effort is integrated into a unified whole";[1] "the joint and continuously integrated effort of two or more specialists having a different disciplinary background";[2] "the internal and substantive interlinking of the various disciplinary analyses so that each considers the results of the others in its own development."[3] Among other things, integrated research benefits from multiple perspectives on the same issues, creation of new avenues for teaching and research, productive interaction with colleagues, and breakdown of disciplinary biases.

Multidisciplinary research, in contrast, involves researchers from different disciplines who are working independently on related problems. Rossini et al. define multidisciplinary research as having external links only,[4] while Birnbaum writes that multidisciplinary scholars are "joined together externally through editorial linkages."[5] Further, Epton et al. note that the literature on interdisciplinary and multidisciplinary work often involves a subtle bias against multidisciplinary work, as if interdisciplinary work is always preferable.[6] Sherif and Sherif write as early as 1969 that "talking about problems of interdisciplinary relationships is a mark of being one of the 'in-crowd.' In the current lingo, it is almost as prestigious to use the term *interdisciplinary* as to speak of being *knowledgeable*."[7]

In contrast, Epton et al. suggest that some research is best suited to a mixture of multi- and interdisciplinary work, moving back and forth along a continuum between the two forms.[8] Some stages (defining the problem and reporting to the public) are more integrated; others (conducting the actual research) are done on a multidisciplinary level. They write, "a more interdisciplinary form is likely to be more appropriate in the early stages of project identification and formulation but may not necessarily be correct at later stages."[9] They describe these hybrid projects as "cross-disciplinary," a term which characterizes the ATC experience better than either of the two extremes of "interdisciplinary" or "multidisciplinary." For example, early in the project, team members worked closely together to develop the overall program, to share knowledge about the fishing industry and communities, to coordinate field work, and to write literature reviews. As predicted by Epton et al., however, once data collection began, the individual members grew apart in response to the demands and divergent needs of the various projects.

The decline in ATC integration may be attributed to constraints in time, geography, and academic culture, as well as to the lack of a suitable reward system, a single "research problem," and defined leadership and organizational structure. These obstacles echo observations by other researchers about problems in interdisciplinary projects. A discussion of these constraints as they apply to ATC follows.

### Integrated research requires an early investment in time, money, planning, and effort in order to create cohesion and overcome differences in disciplinary cultures and terminology.[10]

Creating an integrated team means creating a new culture with common language, values, and goals. ATC participants did not feel that this culture was ever fully developed, for many reasons. There were times, however, when ATC members felt relatively close and integrated. These included conferences, meetings, and workshops when ATC was presented as a group effort. Many participants said that the early series of coastal workshops helped them get to know the other participants and contributed to a more teamlike atmosphere.

### Integrated research requires the willingness of individuals to subordinate their individual interests to a common objective.[11]

This is a fundamental requirement for integration. Because ATC's interdisciplinary goals and tasks were vague, participants had different expectations from the start. Some participants were significantly more willing than others to devote extra effort to fostering integration. This range of responses resulted from differing expectations and career goals rather than from a lack of support for interdisciplinary research. There are often disincentives for nontenured researchers to participate in nontraditional, integrated research. In addition, most participants had little time to devote to developing ATC's team culture. Tenured and nontenured alike were concerned with teaching, publishing, attending professional meetings, procuring funds for future projects, pursuing other research interests, and balancing their personal lives with their careers. The time for developing and sustaining the team culture had not been programmed into individual project work plans or budgets.

### Researchers should be in close physical proximity (preferably on the same floor of the same building).[12]

Proximity promotes the breakdown of disciplinary barriers, creation of a team culture, sharing of data, and other communication. The same-floor requirement seems more feasible for industry than for academia, which typically houses disciplines in different buildings. In the ATC project, the researchers and graduate students were usually located on the campus of Oregon State University, but other participants, including the fishing family coordinators and Extension agents, were located in different towns, sometimes hundreds of miles away. It was very difficult to bring all of the participants (even those located on campus) together for regular meetings.

## Integrated research works best with a small group of researchers (preferably five or six for an academic team).[13]

Whereas there were only 8 principal investigators in ATC, there were at least 29 people, including graduate students, Extension agents, fishing family coordinators, and associate researchers, who qualified as ATC team members. This large membership, combined with their geographical distribution, made it extremely difficult to meet as a group and to develop the necessary bonds for integrated research. The wide variety of participants' backgrounds, from tenured professors to fishermen's wives, increased the challenge of creating a team culture.

## There must be an evaluation and reward structure for interdisciplinary work.[14]

Although there are examples of successfully integrated projects in academia, traditional academic culture does not reward faculty for participating in integrated research projects at the same rate that it rewards them for working inside their own disciplines. At times, there are active disincentives to branch out into interdisciplinary work. Tenure-track faculty feel an imperative to publish, but publishing in interdisciplinary journals is difficult (since there are few of them) and those publications may not be recognized by their departments. In some departments, tenured faculty are also discouraged from "wasting their efforts" on projects outside their discipline.

The ATC project presented a particular challenge to publication-hungry faculty. By design, many ATC publications were written for nonacademic audiences such as fishing family members and fishery managers. This gray literature, which is not peer reviewed, is rarely accepted by tenure review committees on an equal footing with academic publications in scholarly journals.

Academic culture influences integrated work in other ways as well. Because interdisciplinary research is nontraditional and "unproven," integrated research projects dissuade some researchers from participating. On the other hand, they sometimes draw innovative faculty and graduate students who recognize the benefits of this type of cooperative work.[15] Faculty's willingness to work on an interdisciplinary project, and their relationships when they are working on one, may also be influenced by status differences between departments and traditional competitiveness between disciplines. Cultural differences between the "hard" and "soft" sciences, the humanities and the arts pose particular challenges to cooperation.

## Integrated research requires a problem that lends itself to interdisciplinary study.

The ATC project explored a broadly defined research area: that a necessary precondition to achieving sustainable use of fisheries is to understand their human components, including the commercial fishing families, businesses, communities, and economies. This broadness allowed researchers from different disciplines to focus on different problems and different scales (regions, state and federal government, communities, fishing businesses, and families) within the issue of fishing resource decline, rather than different aspects of the same specific research question. An example of a subject that lends itself to a more integrated project might be responses to resource restrictions in commercial fisheries by regions, communities, and families. Each researcher would use the findings by other team members as input into their own project, while supplying their own data to the other project participants. In the ATC model, researchers could (and did) work independently, pursuing the objectives of their own projects without needing to consult with others or provide data.

## Integration must be a clearly defined goal of the research.

Partly because the deadline for the proposal was tight and thus ATC's development process took place quickly, the participants had different views of how integrated the project was meant to be and how integrated they wanted it to be. A summary for the May 15, 1995 ATC meeting states, "A major objective of the past two meetings was to establish a program structure and networking process that would ensure an integrated program consisting of six research projects and a regional outreach project." A model in the original proposal outlined how the researchers and outreach would work together. The participants gradually abandoned this model as the project progressed.

In interviews, participants said they had different perceptions of how ATC would operate. Four interviewees said that they expected and wanted the project to be more integrated, with more intense communication and cooperation, while four said they expected a multidisciplinary project where work was done independently. Two of the latter group said they preferred

ATC to be a less integrated project, while one would have preferred a more integrated project. A majority of the researchers said that when they became involved, they were unsure of how they were going to work together.

### Integrated research requires a team leader whose time is solely devoted to the research team (combining the talents of "ringmaster, bridge scientist, gatekeeper, boundary agent, ombudsman, polymath, dynamo, meta-scientist, specialist/ generalist, and strong entrepreneur").[16]

The literature refers extensively to the importance of the "bridge scientist" who is familiar with all participating disciplines and who coordinates, encourages, develops links, and promotes communication. In ATC, different people came forward at different times to fulfill specific tasks, such as developing ideas for the research project, coordinating proposals, organizing meetings, and encouraging communication. However, in part because of the structure of Sea Grant and the university, there was no single person who was solely devoted to program leadership.

### Integrated research requires an egalitarian, rather than authoritarian, structure.[17]

Sea Grant's administration of the ATC project was neither authoritarian nor completely egalitarian. Although the project was funded by Sea Grant, the organizational structure was created by the researchers in cooperation with Sea Grant staff. Because Sea Grant hoped that internal leadership would arise, it mandated few rules of participation; thus, participants were relatively autonomous. Sea Grant staff provided facilitation and communication support rather than taking on leadership of ATC.

Several participants said they were pleased with Sea Grant's hands-off management style and its flexibility regarding their shifting budgets, methodologies, publications, research goals, and timeliness. This flexibility allowed projects to be responsive to current, unforeseen needs. Some principal investigators, particularly those who were familiar with Sea Grant's management style, were grateful for this independence and the ability to work without constant oversight from management. They also appreciated the personal attention they received from Sea Grant's director and the opportunity to work on a unique and progressive project.

Others, who had less experience with Sea Grant, were unsure of how invested the management expected them to be. One researcher who expected the ATC project to be highly integrated expressed a fear of not meeting Sea Grant's expectations of involvement. Another was unsure of Sea Grant's expectations regarding attendance of non-ATC meetings and functions.

Interviews offered several suggestions for improving ATC's management process. Participants referred to the existing management process as "herding cats" and "pushing elephants" because of the independence of the researchers and associates. While they appreciated this autonomy, many felt that clearer expectations and guidelines would have been helpful from the start of the project. Those who favored a more integrated project felt that willingness to commit to the integration process should have been a prerequisite. Some felt that management should have been more structured and suggested performance measures or timelines with regular, mandatory reporting of progress and results.

## There must be a high level of communication (both formal and informal) and interaction among team members.[18]

The benefits of communication in interdisciplinary research are clear. Communication helps build team culture, reduces misunderstandings, provides data to other researchers, reduces duplication of effort, and acts as a catalyst for creativity.

The majority of ATC participants felt that increased communication would have benefited the project. Although there were attempts to have regular meetings, particularly in the early stages of the project, it was difficult to get everyone together to talk. In the meetings, the principal investigators gave updates on their research progress and discussed future collaborative projects. Most interviewees felt that reserving meeting time for brainstorming and developing links between the projects would have been more effective. Updates could have been provided to each other in other ways, for example, using the Internet or electronic mail groups.

Strictly voluntary communication measures run the risk of being neglected or ignored. Although Sea Grant created an e-mail discussion group to promote communication and a working Web page to be used as a bulletin board for project participants, these media were rarely used. Such lack of communication among projects and ATC members led to missed opportunities, duplication of effort, investment in projects that were later abandoned, lack of knowledge about decisions made at missed meetings, and widening differences in perceptions of the project. Some participants expressed a feeling of ignorance regarding others' projects and disciplines; others felt that their projects weren't sufficiently acknowledged. This communication deficit sprang from the same obstacles that hindered the integration process: differing expectations, differing levels of commitment, and competing demands on time.

## Conclusion

A truly integrated product results from an integrated team of researchers with a common group culture, a tradition of close communication and proximity, and a strong commitment to combining the multiple facets of an interdisciplinary problem into a seamless product. ATC's challenge lay in its participants' differing views on integration. Because the ATC project developed rapidly, no specific plan was created for coordinating the program or developing products other than those proposed in the individual projects.

As the individual ATC projects ended, team members focused on outcomes and results. They continued to value integration, and many wanted to develop integrated outcomes in addition to their own research products. Indeed, some ATC researchers invested integration with symbolic importance and felt that the integration of project outcomes should be a measure of the project's success. However, ATC never developed a fully integrated outcome that involved all of its members.

Pure interdisciplinary work is extremely demanding, particularly in an academic setting where disciplines are physically and culturally separate. Although an interdisciplinary perspective is informative, the ATC project benefits from a cross-disciplinary perspective. Cross-disciplinary work is a dialectical process that moves between full integration and independence. It is a more flexible and forgiving model that the interdisciplinary one in that it does not require total commitment and exacting circumstances. ATC moved along the cross-disciplinary continuum with commendable results. The project produced effective outreach publications, academic and technical reports, conference presentations, and workshops, and the outreach and extension projects fulfilled ATC's goal of helping fishing families, communities, and businesses.

Six years after the ATC idea was first explored, ATC researchers continue to cooperate on publications and outreach projects. Despite the fact that ATC never achieved full integration, most of the participants felt it was an effective project. ATC should provide an important link between its precursor, the Timber Dependent Families Project, and future projects aimed at helping natural resource communities adapt to change.

# Notes

1. P. H. Birnbaum, as quoted by S. R. Epton, R. L. Payne, and A. W. Pearson, Multidisciplinary, Interdisciplinary—What Is the Difference? p. 3 in S. R. Epton, R. L. Payne, and A. W. Pearson, eds., 1983, *Managing Interdisciplinary Research* (Chichester: John Wiley and Sons).

2. A. R. Michaelis, as quoted by S. R. Epton, et al., 1983, Multidisciplinary, Interdisciplinary—What Is the Difference? p. 4.

3. F. A. Rossini, A. L. Porter, D. E. Chubin, and T. Connolly, 1983, Cross-Disciplinarity in the Biomedical Sciences: A Preliminary Analysis of Anatomy, p. 177 in Epton, et al., *Managing Interdisciplinary Research*.

4. Rossini et al. 1983.

5. P. H. Birnbaum, as quoted by Epton et al., 1983, Multidisciplinary, Inter-disciplinary—What Is the Difference? p. 3.

6. Epton et al., 1983, Multidisciplinary, Interdisciplinary—What Is the Difference?

7. M. Sherif and C. W. Sherif, 1969, Interdisciplinary Coordination as a Validity Check: Retrospect and Prospects, pp. 3–20 in M. Sherif and C. W. Sherif, eds., *Interdisciplinary Relationships in the Social Sciences* (Chicago: Aldine).

8. Epton et al. 1983, Multidisciplinary, Interdisciplinary—What Is the Difference?

9. Epton et al. 1983, Multidisciplinary, Interdisciplinary—What Is the Difference? p. 39.

10. Epton et al. 1983, Multidisciplinary, Interdisciplinary—What Is the Difference?; B. O. Saxberg and W. T. Newell, 1983, Interdisciplinary Research in the University: Need for Managerial Leadership, pp. 202–210 in Epton et al., *Managing Interdisciplinary Research*.

11. J. T. Klein and A. L. Porter, 1990, Preconditions for Interdisciplinary Research, pp. 11–19 in P. H. Birnbaum-More, F. A. Rossini, and D. R. Baldwin, eds., *International Research Management* (New York: Oxford University Press).

12. I. L. White, 1975, Interdisciplinarity, pp. 380–387 in S. Arnstein and A. N. Christakis, eds., *Perspectives on Technology Assessment* (Washington, D.C.: Academy for State and Local Governments); Saxberg and Newell 1983.

13. Klein and Porter 1990.

14. S. E. Gold and H. J. Gold, 1983, Some Elements of a Model to Improve Productivity of Interdisciplinary Groups, pp. 86–101 in Epton et al., *Managing Interdisciplinary Research*.

15. Saxberg and Newell 1983.

16. Klein and Porter 1990, p. 14.

17. Klein and Porter 1990.

18. Saxberg and Newell 1983.

# Contributors

**JAN AUYONG** currently serves as assistant director for programs for Oregon Sea Grant at Oregon State University. Facilitation of multidisciplinary and collaborative projects remains a challenging but rewarding part of her work for Sea Grant, along with developing and monitoring resource management and development projects.

**CHRISTOPHER BARKER** is an anthropologist and marine affairs specialist, whose interests are in identity formations and transformations.

**ROLLIE BARNABY** has been with the University of New Hampshire Cooperative Extension/Sea Grant program since 1988. Before that he worked as a teacher, a lobsterman, a restaurateur, and the owner of a retail-wholesale seafood business. He has been on the board of directors of both the New Hampsire Port Authority and the New England Fisheries Development Foundation and has served as president of the Portsmouth Fishermen's Cooperative and as a member of the Sea Grant Policy Advisory Committee.

As an Extension Sea Grant faculty member at Oregon State University, **FLAXEN D. L. CONWAY** works with coastal communities and families who are affected by changes in natural resource policy and management. She helps access resources, build coalitions, and plan strategies that meet the needs of all interests. In partnership with other subject matter specialists and Extension agents, she provides coastal and statewide outreach for the development of program and educational materials related to conflict transformation, community economic development, and managing change.

**JOSEPH CONE** is the assistant director for communications of Oregon Sea Grant, the head of the office that supports the Sea Grant program with communications products. Cone was the Sea Grant science writer from 1983 to 1994. Recently, he has specialized in producing material relating to salmon retoration in the Pacific Northwest, including writing a book, *A Common Fate,* coediting a documentary history, *The Northwest Salmon Crisis,* producing a videotape, the *Return of the Salmon,* and editing a newsletter, *Restoration.*

**LORI A. CRAMER** is an associate professor of sociology, specializing in environmental and natural resource sociology. Her interests broadly concern the application of sociology to natural resource problems, with an emphasis on conducting social impact assessments (e.g., determining how a community perceives potential changes to its environment). Cramer has conducted assessments ranging from siting hazardous facilities to siting ski resorts near rural communities. She is currently studying how fishing families and communities along the Oregon coast are adapting to social change.

**JOHN GATES** is a professor of environmental and natural resource economics at the University of Rhode Island. He specializes in marine resource policy.

**JENNIFER GILDEN** has been studying the social dimensions of natural resource issues since 1993. Her work has focused on the interactions between humans and salmon in the Pacific Northwest, and on how families are adapting to economic and cultural change in timber and commercial fishing communities. She is also co-founder of the Institute for Culture and Ecology, a nonprofit research organization in Portland, Oregon.

**MADELEINE HALL-ARBER,** an anthropologist with the Massachusetts Institute of Technology's Sea Grant College Program, specializes in the analysis of social impacts of regulatory change in fisheries management. She serves on the New England Fishery Management Council's Social Science Advisory Committee, the Atlantic States Marine Fisheries Commission's Committee on Economics and Social Sciences, and several technical committees. Six years ago she founded an international e-mail list, FISHFOLK, for discussion of social science issues in fisheries.

**SUSAN HANNA** is professor of marine economics at Oregon State University. She researches economic dimensions of fishery management to understand the interaction of economic incentives, decision making, and management performance in marine ecosystems. She advises the Pacific Fishery Management Council, Northwest Power Planning Council, National Marine Fisheries Service, and National Oceanic and Atmospheric Administration. She has been a member of the National Research Council's Ocean Studies Board and several NRC Committees, including the Committee to Review Individual Quotas in Fisheries.

Prior to her appointment at OSU, **LAURIE HOUSTON** spent several years working with economic incentives and natural resource policy issues. As a faculty research assistant at Oregon State University, she has worked with Rebecca Johnson on various economic impact studies associated with forestry, recreation, and tourism.

**REBECCA JOHNSON** teaches classes on the economics of recreation resources and conducts research on the economics of nonmarketed forest resources. Past research includes nonmarket valuation using the contingent valuation and travel cost methods, and economic impact estimation using input-output models. She currently serves on the governor's Council of Economic Advisors for the State of Oregon.

**LORI A. MCGRAW** is a doctoral candidate in the Department of Human Development and Family Sciences at Oregon State University. She teaches courses in relationship and family development and was a counselor for 10 years before returning to graduate school. She studies individual and family development, using feminist theories and qualitative methodologies.

**MARGARET MANOOGIAN-O'DELL** is a Ph.D. student in the Human Development and Family Studies program at Oregon State University. Under the direction of Anisa Zvonkovic, she worked as a member of a research team that examined the impact of the fishing industry on families with children.

An associate professor of sociology at the University of Rhode Island, **HELEN J. MEDERER** examines the intersection of work and family life. She has spent the past six years studying the changes in families caused by changing regulations of commercial fishing. Earlier, she studied wives of Naval submariners, and the family roles of female state workers. She is working on a book that describes how gender conceptions and identities are being affected by the transformations in commercial fishing families.

**HANS RADTKE** has a courtesy faculty appointment at Oregon State University and is a recognized leader in input/output analysis and natural recourse economics. As a freelance economist, he has worked on a variety of projects relating to the fishing industry for the Oregon Department of Fish and Wildlife, the Pacific Fishery Management Council, the West Coast and Alaska fisheries, and for Oregon Coastal Zone Management Association.

**R. BRUCE RETTIG** is a professor of agricultural and resource economics at Oregon State University. He has served on advisory committees for several fishery agencies, including the Pacific Fishery Management Council, the Northwest Power Planning Council, and the Food and Agricluture Organizaiton of the United Nations. In addition, he has parrticipated in many international discussions of fishery management. Currently, he is completing a research project on the role of compensation as a tool to address salmon crises.

**COURTLAND L. SMITH** is a cultural anthropologist, who earned his Ph.D. at the University of Arizona. He has adjunct appointments in the Department of Fisheries and Wildlife and the College of Oceanography at Oregon State University. Smith has a long-term interest in Pacific Northwest salmon problems, writing *Salmon Fishers of the Columbia,* published by the Oregon State University Press in 1979.

**BRENT S. STEEL** is an associate professor of political science and director of the Program for Governmental Research and Education at Oregon State University. The author, coauthor, or editor of over 60 journal articles, book chapters, and books, he received a B.A. in economics and government from Eastern Washington University and an M.A. and a Ph.D. in political science from Washington State University.

**ED WATERS,** an economist with the Oregon Legislative Revenue Office, also has a courtesy faculty appointment at Oregon State University. He specializes in the analysis of regional tax and resource management issues. As a self-employed contractor he has worked for OSU, Oregon Sea Grant, and the Western Rural Development Center. His projects have included economic analyses of the impact of fishery recovery measures on Oregon coastal communities and on the role of resource-based industries in the Oregon and Washington economies.

**ANISA M. ZVONKOVIC** is an associate professor in the Department of Human Development and Family Sciences at Oregon State University. She received her M.S. and Ph.D. degrees in human development and family studies at Pennsylvania State University. Her research interests include work and family issues, intimacy, and close relationship dynamics.

# Index